W9-AEP-333

PRAISE FOR REGINA LEEDS

"Making your New Year's resolutions? If your goal is to finally clear the clutter, *One Year to an Organized Life* will break the task down week by week."

—*Parade*

"The perfect book for anyone wanting to find important papers instantly or have a navigable closet. Full of useful information for everyone, from the person who needs simply to clean a messy desk to the person requiring a whole new approach to life; highly recommended."

—*Library Journal* on *One Year to an Organized Life*

"[Leeds's] advice is simple, practical, and essential. . . . Calm and empowering, this handy guide is so well thought-out that just leafing through the pages might make you feel more in control."

—*Boston Globe* on *One Year to an Organized Financial Life*

"Readers should find plenty of smart, straightforward and re-warding ways to eliminate chaos from their work lives."

—*Publishers Weekly* on *One Year to an Organized Work Life*

"Leeds covers it all. Week-by-week tasks provide clear, real-istic goals for the determined mother-to-be, and some weeks involve simply thinking about organizing or creating routines. The emphasis here is on the difficult choices that have to be made, and the logistics behind making them. Leeds will likely change the thinking of many a would-be parent: being orga-nized is actually far easier than the alternative."

—*Publishers Weekly* on *One Year to an Organized Life with Baby*

"Leeds gets right to the point and offers simple, attainable advice."

—*Library Journal* on *The 8 Minute Organizer*

DISCARD

RIGHTSIZE . . .
RIGHT NOW!

Also by Regina Leeds

The 8 Minute Organizer

One Year to an Organized Life with Baby (with Meagan Francis)

One Year to an Organized Financial Life (with Russell Wild)

One Year to an Organized Work Life

One Year to an Organized Life

The Complete Idiot's Guide to Decluttering

Sharing a Place Without Losing Your Space

The Zen of Organizing

RIGHTSIZE . . .
RIGHT NOW!

The Eight-Week Plan to Organize,
Declutter, and Make Any Move Stress-Free

REGINA LEEDS

Da Capo
LIFE
LONG

A Member of the Perseus Books Group

Copyright © 2015 by Regina Leeds
"The Zen of Organizing" and "Zen Organizer" are registered trademarks
of Regina Leeds.

All rights reserved. No part of this publication may be reproduced,
stored in a retrieval system, or transmitted, in any form or by any means,
electronic, mechanical, photocopying, recording, or otherwise, without
the prior written permission of the publisher. Printed in the United
States of America. For information, address Da Capo Press,
44 Farnsworth Street, 3rd Floor, Boston, MA 02210

Designed by Linda Mark
Set in 10.5 point Guardi LT Std by the Perseus Books Group

Library of Congress Cataloging-in-Publication Data
Leeds, Regina.
  Rightsize . . . right now! : the eight-week plan to organize, declutter,
and make any move stress-free / Regina Leeds.
     pages cm
  Includes index.
  ISBN 978-0-7382-1801-4 (paperback)—ISBN 978-0-7382-1802-1
(e-book) 1. Moving, Household. 2. Orderliness. I. Title. II. Title: Right
size . . . right now!

  TX307.L434 2015
  648'.9—dc23

                                                         2014039459

First Da Capo Press edition 2015

Published by Da Capo Press
A Member of the Perseus Books Group
www.dacapopress.com

Da Capo Press books are available at special discounts for bulk
purchases in the U.S. by corporations, institutions, and other
organizations. For more information, please contact the Special
Markets Department at the Perseus Books Group, 2300 Chestnut
Street, Suite 200, Philadelphia, PA, 19103, or call (800) 810-4145,
ext. 5000, or e-mail special.markets@perseusbooks.com.

10 9 8 7 6 5 4 3 2 1

R0443326758

For Charlie and all the companion animals
who have so generously graced my life.
I am humbled by your ability to love, forgive, and inspire.

Until one has loved an animal
a part of one's soul remains unawakened.

—ANATOLE FRANCE

CONTENTS

INTRODUCTION

Whatever you can do,
or dream you can, begin it.
Boldness has genius
power and magic in it.

—GOETHE

TAKE A MINUTE TO SEARCH THE INTERNET FOR THE MOST stressful life experiences you can have, and you'll discover moving on that list, along with death, divorce, major illness, and job loss. I presume you have a move on the horizon and may be dealing with sleepless nights, eating binges, and temper tantrums. Moving causes physical, emotional, and mental upheaval. One minute you're fine and dandy, living in a house or apartment, and the next, for any number of reasons, you need to change residences. Even a move for positive reasons, such as recent nuptials or a promotion, can strain nerves. Moves that are foisted on us cause off-the-charts stress. As the calendar days fly by, you find yourself feeling exhausted and practicing the fine art of procrastination. I'm here to help. Let's start with a look at my style of organizing, and then I'll explain how I structured this book for maximum payoff.

Long before I became a professional organizer, I made two moves in one year. The experience of packing, moving, and unpacking—only to do it all again a few months later—was so traumatic that I decided I would forever keep only what I treasured and loved. Neatly tucking things away in closets, the basement, or the back of the garage simply because I had the space and could delay a decision no longer made sense to me. This philosophy requires me to stop every three to five years and have a "nothing is sacred" weekend during which I donate or toss older items that no longer serve me to make room for the things I currently need. I also want to open space for things I might need in the future. Life is always changing and so should our environments. Everything I own is the right size for the home I currently occupy. Is there one "right size" fits all? Absolutely not! Rightsizing takes into consideration what you literally need for the size of your home, your family, and the obligations you have at your current stage of life. The head of a large corporation and your ninety-year-old aunt have different life demands. They should have different amounts of stuff to meet those demands elegantly and efficiently.

Even if your next move is far in the future, you can use this book to rightsize your home. Every few years it's great to reassess what we own and see if it's time to tweak the environment. For example, a few years ago I visited an elderly relative. I noticed that all of my late uncle's things were still in his room, even though he had been gone for more than a decade. He left no wife or children, just his brothers and sisters. I asked if I could sort through his possessions and see what could be donated to charity or tossed. In the process, I was surprised to find usable items still taking up valuable space. For example another sister, recently deceased, had placed a large stash of disposable razors in a plastic bag labeled with the contents and the date. They were in my uncle's dresser along with a myriad collection of other bagged and labeled personal items—as if he were on a long trip and would need everything upon his return. It is amazing how loyal we are to stuff that will never again be used. Today when guests come to visit my aunt, they can make themselves comfortable in my late uncle's old room with closet space, empty drawers, and even a disposable razor for their use. A little organization can go a long way to giving you the livable space you need—so take a step back and consider the things in your home.

Can I stress that point enough, I wonder? You can understand the words and are hopefully touched by my examples, but can you apply them to your situation? It can be tough to look on your possessions with an impartial eye, but you don't ever want your home to feel stale or staid, do you? You want it to be vibrant and alive, just like you are. You loved your college dorm or first apartment, but it would look odd to have the exact same decor when you're fifty. You set up your nursery with great love, but your teenager doesn't even want to see photos of how adorable it was. Time and life march on. We need to keep in step.

The Zen of Organizing

When I was growing up, there were no piles in our home. Everything had its place, and my mother insisted that my father and I return items the second we were done using them—no exceptions. I assumed that everyone lived by the same rules. As a young adult, I didn't realize that friends cleaned up before you came over for a visit—that their homes weren't always company ready. And I was lucky to date men as tidy as I was. (There was one exception, but he later served as fodder for my classes, so I'm grateful for his complete lack of organizing skills. Still, in many ways I felt like I was observing someone from another galaxy.)

When I began to organize people for a living, I saw what a challenge organization can be for many people. My clients laid bare their environments with a mix of vulnerability and fearlessness that opened the door to change. They literally let it all hang out. I heard their excuses, their stories, and their reasons for seeking change. I saw their tax returns and folded their underwear. I had thought organizing was a mechanical skill and discovered it has deep psychological and emotional roots. Digging around in someone's stuff is like reading his or her diary. Organizing another human being is an intimate experience. It's also a privilege. Over time I noticed that a completed space felt tangibly different from when we started. It felt like the home I knew from my childhood and all the environments I had created as an adult. The change created a subtle shift in energy.

When I decided to write a book, I initially aimed to share my knowledge with those I could never meet in person. But what would I call this book? That shift in energy was a huge part of my approach to organization, and I was at a loss for to how to describe it in a simple, catchy title. One day a client said to me, "Oh, you mean it's Zen-like." I knew I had my title (*The Zen of Organizing*, now out of print), my professional title (the Zen Organizer™), and a name for my style of organizing (Zen Organizing™). Funny how things come together when you open yourself to finding the solution.

I describe Zen Organizing as a system that takes into account the emotional, psychological, physical, and spiritual state you find yourself in as you begin an organizing project. I see you as the all-powerful architect of whatever mess now surrounds you, and I urge you to celebrate that reality. If you are the creator of the worst, you are clearly free now to create the best! Zen Organizing works to craft an environment that brings harmony to every part of your being. Most people live in surroundings that sabotage them at every turn; a Zen-Organized home nurtures all inhabitants so that they are free to do the work for which they were born. You can spend your life looking for your keys or you can spend it writing the great American novel or whatever personal pursuit fires your jets.

The Magic Formula

When I began my career as a professional organizer, for the first three years I had sleepless nights each time a new client called. I was convinced he or she would ask me to organize something and I'd have to admit I didn't have a clue. As time passed, however, I noticed that every project yielded to order when I followed the same three steps; all that changed were the types of items in my hands. One day I might be sorting clothing, the next I'd be filing paper, and the week would end with a garage filled with tools. It was all the same process. I called the three steps "the Magic Formula" because of their universal applicability. To this day I have never encountered a project that would not yield when I patiently and logically moved through the formula. Here are the three steps of the Magic Formula:

- Eliminate
- Categorize
- Organize

Elimination is the most creative step in many ways. You get to free items you no longer need or want or will never use to a new life of their own. The old sofa that you kept from your college dorm can now be donated to a charity; the ink-jet printer you haven't used since the laser version entered the home office can go to a day care center in your neighborhood; the clothing from decades ago that will never fit your current body no matter how much weight you lose can go to a women's shelter. There will be items that have no future except the trash can or recycle bin, but that's OK. If you enjoyed them, used them, and have great memories, they served their purpose. These items represent the past. The goal is not to drag them into your future—and this is especially important when rightsizing for your space.

Categorization makes you powerful, gives you immediate inventory control, and allows everyone in the family to know where the chicken soup, toilet paper, or dog treats are simply because they have to be in the one place designated for that type of product. Time is saved, emotional upset is avoided, and money is no longer squandered purchasing items you already have in abundance. You can't beat the power of a category to make your life easier!

Organization is what we do when you've whittled down your entire inventory of stuff to the items you really need to keep. But it's important to eliminate and categorize before setting up your system. If you purchase one hundred hangers before you start organizing your closet for example and discover you only needed sixty, you now either have forty extra hangers creating their own kind of debris, or you have to schlep them back for a refund. That's either wasted space or wasted time and energy. Everyone is instantly on board when it comes to saving money, and I hope you will come to value saving space, energy, and time equally. You can earn more money, make more room, and get some rest, but frittered time is lost forever.

Zen-Organized spaces are beautiful to look at, completely functional, and easy to maintain. At this last juncture in the process, you need the tips and tricks all professional organizers know, as well as an idea of which products are best for the task at hand. I think the best-quality products are at The Container Store, and that's where I'll direct you, but feel free to use my suggestions as nothing more than a creative jumping-off point. If you know where to get something better or cheaper, go for it! I'm not working on commission.

Zen Organizing and Your Move

When it comes to your move, you have a choice. You can leave all the details to the last minute. You can take things with you to the new location that are no longer needed and live with unpacked boxes for a decade. You can wear yourself out and maybe even get sick. Or you can systematically tackle the myriad details such a big project creates and arrive at your new home a little tired but filled with pride in your accomplishment. You can focus not on the upheaval but on the new life that awaits you. Again the choice is yours. You know which one I'm here to help you make.

Time Frame for Rightsizing

I chose eight weeks for this plan because most of us have at least that much time to prepare before any move. If you're lucky and have more time, you can stretch out some of the projects, and if you have less, you can compress the weeks as needed. I've crafted this plan for a typical family moving out of a two-bedroom, two-bathroom house into one of equivalent size, but it can apply to any space. You may find that certain activities don't apply to you, and that will give you more time to do the things that are common to all moves. Not every person has a garage or an attic, for example, but we all have a bedroom and a kitchen. You might be moving to a studio apartment from your parents' home. Or perhaps you just had baby number five and are moving into a six-bedroom house. Don't dismiss the guidelines because your situation is different. That's an unconscious move common to people who want to avoid something and think it's easier to shoot the messenger. "What does she know? That doesn't apply to me!" You can tailor the advice to suit your needs. If you don't currently have a basement, attic, guest room, or garage you can smugly read the material for the suggested tips and then go sit by the pool. Conversely, if you are leaving your mansion for a condo, you can double down and work faster and a wee bit harder. It's all doable in eight weeks' time.

Structure

Each chapter is formulated so that you will have the following:

- After the first week, which is top-heavy with initial research, I have a rightsizing project for every week to help you divest yourself of what you no longer need or want or will never use in the new space. Tackling these decisions at the other end makes no sense; nor does living for years with unpacked boxes. Stacks of anything (papers, boxes, clothing, etc.) are unmade decisions staring you in the face. The visual exhausts you and leaves you feeling guilty. I'd like to expunge such experiences from your life and prevent them from entering the new location. It only takes a little extra elbow grease in the current one.

- In every chapter you'll find call-out boxes with tips you can use to facilitate your move. I've chosen these carefully for their versatility and power. You can use them to get ready for the big day, whether it will happen in eight weeks or at some undetermined future date. You might find these tips motivating and just what you need to galvanize you into action. It's never really possible to predict what the first domino might be. That's a personal matter for every reader.

- There will be tips to help you organize the items you choose to take with you in the new space. Here again we see the power of categories. You know exactly what you need to organize. I presume you know the size and dimensions of the cupboards and drawers in the new space. Armed with that information you can avail yourself of free-space planning at an entity like The Container Store or IKEA. They can design simple organizing systems for your clothes closets, a pantry, or the garage. And, of course, my tips include lists of my favorite organizing tools.

- Chapters conclude with a summary so you can easily reference the material covered. Feel free to copy them into a notebook. And please do tailor them to fit your unique situation and needs. (See more on making your move notebook on page 23.)

- Every chapter has a suggestion for a reward. This is a difficult time, and you need to pat yourself on the back each week and tell yourself, "Job well done!" Morale boosters are key to success. Be sure to extend rewards to family members and devoted friends who are helping you make the transition. Very often the self-care tip for the week can be used as a reward. Anybody up for an aromatherapy bubble bath at the end of a day of work, parenting, and packing boxes? I thought so.

Throughout the book, we'll also look at the particular challenges of specific types of moves, like going to live in a dorm or mini apartment, moving in with relatives when life tosses you a temporary curve ball, or going into assisted living. I wouldn't skip those sections if they don't apply to you because they are choc full of practical tips you might wish to make use of in your situation. I've scattered related material throughout the book. You're on a treasure hunt for the best tips for you.

Read through the book once and then go back and begin your official journey. Make notes in your journal. You'll suddenly be armed with a lot of basic information and will no doubt begin to feel a sense of control replacing the inevitable panic that precedes such a big change. You are free to shift steps from one week to another; however, I would recommend swapping rather than deferring them and then having to tackle multiple assignments the week before the moving truck pulls up in front of your door. Procrastination is not your friend.

SELF-CARE TIP FOR THE WEEK

WHILE SELF-CARE IS always important, it's critical during a move. Now is not the time to stuff your face with Twinkies, cancel your gym membership, stay up all night fretting, or guzzle gallons of soda. It's time to drink lots of water, eat fresh produce, sleep eight hours each night, and get plenty of exercise, even if that just means taking Fido around the block several times a day. You're in training for an event that can open the door to new experiences or put you in bed for several weeks.

The Power of (Good) Habits

As you prepare to launch the next phase of your life in a different location, it's a great time to cultivate good habits. If you do things that cause chaos in the home now, you can tweak your behavior so that by the time you are unpacking, you are automatically in an organized frame of mind. Here is a list of my all-time favorite habits, although the books in the *One Year to . . .* series are chock-full of suggestions.

- Wash dirty dishes (or put them in the dishwasher) immediately rather than leaving them in the sink. A stack of dirty dishes is a depressing visual and represents a big task.
- Put dishes away rather than allowing them to languish on the drain board or sit in the dishwasher. (After you wash a load of dishes, leave the door open for about an hour so the inside of the machine can dry. Bacteria love dark, wet environments. This tip also applies to your washing machine.)
- Make your bed every day.
- Check the trash cans daily, and empty as needed.
- Put your keys in the same spot the second you enter your home. Put up a hook, designate a special dish, or plop them into your

purse. If you constantly lose the remote or your glasses, designate homes for them as well. You'll always know where to look for important items when they have a home.

- Do your paperwork every day at the same time and in the same location. Some tasks simply aren't fun, but when they are regimented a bit, you'll find yourself automatically taking care of them.

Many psychologists say it takes twenty-one consecutive days to create a habit, and it needs to be a repeatable action. It can be tricky to cultivate even the simplest change in your daily life, but once you have a new habit solidified, you will wonder how you lived any other way. I would choose no more than two to start. You don't want to overwhelm yourself. Set yourself up to win!

The Ultimate Helper: A To-Do List

I don't know what I would do without my trusty to-do list. Instead of addressing all the issues in my life that demand attention, my daily list guides me to accomplish only the items I can easily tackle that day. Whether you use an electronic or paper calendar, you'll want to keep track of your personal and work responsibilities, along with the myriad details suddenly clamoring for your attention. I start my suggestions here with an assumption that some kind of scheduling is already a part of your life. Without it, you are apt to forget things and live with more stress than necessary. If you have a photographic memory and rely on it to keep you on track, be warned that over time it's less reliable. I speak from experience.

A good way to start is by reading this book through once, as I suggested, and noting things you need to do, like call a few movers, measure the cupboards and count the drawers in the new home, and order checks imprinted with your new address. When done, you'll have the rudiments of the master list for your move. I know folks who carry their master life list around with them. I can't imagine anything less productive. Being confronted with everything you need to accomplish is overwhelming, even if you are extremely organized. At night, make a to-do list of specific tasks for the next day. Be sure you consider each item carefully: Is it necessary? Is tomorrow the ideal day to tackle it? Factor in how much time a task will realistically take, including travel time. If you drive, allow time for the inevitable parking drama that is part and parcel of life in a big congested city. There's no sin in bumping tasks, although there is trouble on the horizon if you do it continuously. If you procrastinate, you'll end up moving things with you that should find new homes or be tossed. It may take months to recover, when you could be enjoying your new home and neighborhood. Please don't do that to yourself.

As you look at your calendar (I prefer month-at-a-glance), consider whether you could move items to tomorrow from another day. Could doubling your efforts in a specific neighborhood, for example, prevent you from returning the following week? Geographical intelligence will save you time, money, and energy. It's equally important to husband your personal energy. You don't want to bolt out of the starting gate and then flag in week three. Finally, this is a wonderful time to practice the art of saying no. I once checked with a mover to make sure my client's move was on track for the next day. Imagine my surprise when I learned she had rescheduled for the following week. When I asked her why, she told me she had agreed to head a committee at her son's school. She inconvenienced me as well as the movers, and she also denied another parent the opportunity to step up and run the committee. If you feel you do everything better than everyone else on the planet, the period right before a move is the perfect time to disabuse yourself of this notion. Learn to mentor. It's another great life skill.

Seek Help

Even if you wish to do your own move, I would still consult with a large moving company just to get the free literature they provide. You might even be persuaded to let them do the work while you concentrate on downsizing. Help also comes from many surprising sources. For example, when I moved I discovered that a lot of well-known stores in my neighborhood, like West Elm and Pottery Barn, had coupons to help me feather my new nest at a discount.

Also, don't hesitate to call in favors from family members and friends. Instead of issuing a general cry for help, tailor each request to the best person for the job. Never ask someone who is consistently critical of you for help. You know in advance where that's going to lead. Spreading out your requests will ensure that no one will start avoiding your calls or fake a trip to Borneo the weekend of your move. If you have a particularly savvy Internet researcher in the family, ask him or her to find things and people you need, like local charities that will make a pickup or someone to sell items on eBay for you. If you lack a skilled family member or friend, you might want to hire a virtual assistant to take these details off your to-do list. We'll talk more about those later. In your move notebook (a must!), you can make notes as you read so you are on top of the information you need to secure.

Perhaps you are moving to a new city and have children who are less than thrilled about this turn of events. If so, help them find outlets in the new location for the things that matter most to them. We can get so lost in our grief that we forget to direct our energy to a solution. Knowing that other kids their age in the new location are equally passionate about Lego, American Girl dolls, tennis, politics, or cooking can soothe an angry child or teenager. You'll want to know where your favorite grocery stores and a great dry cleaner are located. I was overwhelmed when I realized that a simple eight-mile move in the same city meant changing almost every store I used. Thank heaven for chains!

We get so caught up in learning the best way to pack items like dishes or books that we forget we also need to fill the gap made by leaving behind our network of family and friends. That loss is part of what makes a move such an emotional experience. A trained monkey can pack a box of books, but no one can replace your best friend. On the other hand, other people your age will surely be facing the same loss in your new location, and you can connect with them. Social media are a boon in this quest at the same time that they so beautifully keep us connected to our current tribe. Only the willingness to reach out is required. I made a long-distance move across the United States long before social media hit the scene. It's a daunting task to make new friends; you need to remember that it takes time and effort. That makes packing boxes seem like the easy part, doesn't it?

Why Am I So Tired?

The most exhausting part of any organizing project—and let's face it, moving is the mother of all organizing projects—is the fatigue that sets in with making decisions. In fact, we in organizing circles use the phrase "decision fatigue" because we see it in our clients on a regular basis. My recent move happened because I fell in love with a puppy and was told he would not be welcome at my current residence. Yes, I downsized and moved for the love of a dog. I was a bit cocky about my ability to do it without a lot of help. After all, don't I do this for a living? For several months I did indeed go it all alone. I looked for a new apartment. I downsized. I packed up the unbreakable items to save money. I unpacked in the new space. And as often as I could, I visited my puppy at the home of a friend who had agreed to watch him for me. About twenty-four hours after the movers left, I hit the proverbial wall. I could do everything left on my to-do list except figure out how to cover the windows. The owner had stripped them bare, and I was living in a fish bowl. I had no privacy and a bad case of decision fatigue. Suddenly the very idea of choosing between blinds, drapes, curtains, or any other type of window dressing was beyond my ability. A great friend rushed to help, and in short order my windows were covered, I completed setting up the new space, and little Charlie moved in.

Tell Me Your Story

I have a doctor who says those words the minute she walks into the exam room. It's a great icebreaker, and we always start with a good laugh. It's my turn to ask you a slightly different version of this question: What is the story of your move? You're probably thinking along the lines of a linear response: "Well, Regina, I'm in a two-bedroom, one-bathroom apartment with my husband, and we just found out I'm pregnant so we bought a house. That's my move story." Those are the facts, but I want to know your story. Do you expect an easy move? Are you blessed with family and friends who you are sure will show up to help? What about past moves? Were they traumatic or a boatload of fun? It's your belief system that continuously re-creates your story until you give it new direction. Let me give you an example.

Carla is going from one rental house to another. A series of bad real estate investments caused her to lose everything in the financial crash of 2008. Now she has lost her roommates and will need to rehome most of her pets. She insists on renting large spaces to accommodate her collection of stuff that includes furniture, clothing in several sizes, her late mother's belongings, and outdated paperwork going back well beyond the time of interest to Uncle Sam. When anyone suggests that she downsize to a smaller space until she's back on her feet financially, she angrily and unconsciously begins to tell her story. It's one of loss, failure, and betrayal and has nothing to do with present circumstances, but it rules her. In psychology this might be termed "a consciousness of lack or loss." It is typical of people who believe they will always lose.

In contrast, I have another friend who was once married to a famous actor and lived the life we all see in magazines. I met Ruth well after her divorce and discovered in passing that she had been married. When I asked her what had happened, she smiled and said that although she hadn't told her story in years, she would make an exception for me. I learned her husband had cheated on her and left her for another woman. For a year she talked about the betrayal and upheaval to anyone who would listen. She said she woke up one day and realized that if she didn't change her story, her life would never be whole again. After she shared what happened, she told me she would never speak of him or that time again to anyone. She wanted to live in the now, not as a slave to the past. I have enormous respect for Ruth and made a note to emulate her. I had no idea at that time that her story might inspire others to let go. I'm so grateful she made an exception for me.

If your impending move is cloaked in negative past experiences, I promise you things will not go well. We create what we expect. Perhaps you're given to negative experiences and frequently exclaim, "I knew that was going to happen. Things never turn out well for me," or "What did you expect? This is how it is for people in our family." There are hundreds of variations on the song, and if you sing it in honor of your move, no amount of planning will help you. You expect the worst, and the worst will re-create itself for you with amazing fidelity. The best mover in the world and an army of professional organizers will be powerless to give you a good experience. You don't feel you deserve it. We need to change that so that your move ushers in a fresh start that encompasses more than your new physical address.

BENEFITS OF DOWNSIZING

There are many benefits to downsizing, and if you embrace them, the task will be easier. To wit:

- A smaller home means lower bills, which might allow you to save or enjoy more leisure activities like travel.
- Upkeep is easier, which means you save time and energy.
- If you move to an urban area, you might be able to eliminate one or both cars and use public transportation. Cars can always be rented for special occasions. Between gas, registration, insurance, and maintenance, a car eats into your disposable income. In a city, you can take advantage of museums, restaurants, and go sightseeing using public transportation.

Words of Caution

Some people hear an instruction and instantly embrace the idea behind it. They shoot themselves in the foot, however, by engaging in a fruitless quest for the perfect way to implement the solution. I've seen clients download numerous apps and buy countless types of calendars looking for the one that will best serve them. I've seen people abandon perfectly good solutions because they got caught up in how to cross-reference material far beyond the personal need at hand. And heaven help those among you who love to create spreadsheets. Creating the perfect spreadsheet can become a task unrelated to anything you have to accomplish. Self-sabotage comes in many forms. Spend no more than a day looking for the perfect app, the greatest notebook, or the best way to use both. Ask friends and family what they use if you don't have your tools in place. You know what Nike says: just do it! This is life advice, not just instruction for your move.

Begin your day with the intention to get things done, and don't be timid about practicing one of the most powerful life skills you can learn: say no! Saying yes to one favor requested by a friend, co-worker, or loved one can derail your day. It's always important to protect your time; doing so is critical in the weeks before your move. Don't think a denial makes you a bad or selfish person. Clearly if a friend asks for a ride to the hospital, you're going to drop everything. But small tasks can take you away from the work you need to accomplish over the next eight weeks. In fact, you may be the one asking for favors during this period! Saying no is very difficult for many of my clients, so I understand if you are recoiling in horror at the very idea. Here's my promise: no one will die if you can't help out, and the person looking for the favor will move on to someone else. Anyone who becomes angry with you is probably prone to using others to get things done in his or her own life. You can live without that pressure. Moving is an opportunity for a fresh start on every level.

A Closing Thought

Unpacking a client is one of the most creative experiences I have in my profession. You need to buckle down and do your homework, but your move can open the door to incredible creativity, newfound freedom, and the next chapter in your life, whether you're going off to college, getting ready to spend your third act in a retirement community, or enjoying one of the myriad phases of life in between. Life is always what we make it, and moving doesn't have to make you chronically fatigued, bitchy, or ill.

MAKE A PLAN

The moment one definitely commits oneself, then
Providence moves, too.

—W. H. Murray, "The Scottish Himalayan Expedition"

THIS WEEK WE BEGIN THE MARCH TO YOUR NEW HOME. NO
matter the nature of this move, I hope you will embrace the possibilities inherent in any type of transition. Think of the fable of two young children who returned home from school and found mounds of horse manure in their respective front yards. One child wondered what all this manure was doing in his yard. He was perplexed, confused, and angry. The other child looked at the manure and squealed in delight: "Where's the pony?" Let's keep our eyes peeled for that pony, shall we?

For any big project, preparation is key, so this week you'll focus on doing your research and making a plan. Many of you are going to use professional movers, and I'm here to help you find a reputable and experienced company. You can't move with or without a pro, however, until you know what your moving budget is, so this week you'll also put together your financial forecast.

You want to create a move notebook as the official repository of all your notes. (No more scrambling from room to room, wailing, "I know I had that Post-it in my hand just this morning.")

There are other items on our to-do list this week, but these are the big-ticket items. Moving tends to cause many people to freeze with fear. We're facing that fear down this week with a simple exercise: a single item designated for donation, recycling, or the trash can be all that's needed to get the ball rolling. You know what they say: once the first domino falls, the rest are sure to follow! And now let's roll up our sleeves and get started, shall we?

The Solution Is in the Details

By nature I am a procrastinator, as are many of us. We all race to do the things we love. The things we dread, however, can really cause us to drag our feet. You won't be surprised to learn that my mother never let me put off to the last minute any school project that caused me discomfort. Now, with a heart filled with gratitude for my mother, the most organized human being and my mentor, I offer the same advice to you. You need to make a plan because while eight weeks sounds like an eternity, it's going to pass in a flash. You don't want to be up all night the evening before the movers arrive to move your stuff, right? That happened to me once years before I became a professional organizer. You'd be surprised how your possessions go from "precious mementos" to "trash" as the hours fly by before the truck shows up.

Remember, the plan was crafted for a typical two-bedroom, two-bathroom home, but the same eight-week structure applies whether you're moving out of an apartment or a mansion. This week we'll take the first two critical steps in your plan, gather some tools, and make a dent. Are you ready?

The Moving Mantra

We all get overwhelmed when we look at the big picture. People come to hear me speak and leave fired up to get organized. They go home intent on setting up a great file system or making their closet look like a boutique in Milan—then the reality hits. The closet is stacked to the rafters with clothing, shoes, and miscellaneous items; the office looks like the FBI just did a raid. As the literal door closes, so does the one inside their hearts that had opened up to a new reality. I'll get organized some other time, they think. But wait! It doesn't have to be like this.

You succeed by breaking things down into manageable chunks. You aren't organizing the entire office—you're tackling the desk. And you aren't doing the entire desk, just the stack of papers to your left. And you aren't even going to organize that big stack in one action. You're going to decide the fate of each piece of paper, one at a time. The same strategy applies to any project, including this move. The very idea of moving may send you screaming from the room straight to that box of ice cream waiting in the freezer. But I don't want you to arrive in your new home with an extra five pounds on your hips! When feeling overwhelmed, here's all you have to repeat to yourself: "Regina said it would be like this. I need to focus on one detail at a time." Take a deep breath and find the detail you can tackle.

Preparation Is Key

This is where I sound like your mother. Here's a list of things that will take you easily over the finish line. They will make your life better every day, and you'll experience that ease and support as you use these tools to facilitate your move. Today I have to say, "Trust me." On moving day, you'll be telling everyone how you have managed to stay so calm.

What does the Zen Organizer suggest you remain vigilant about over the next eight weeks?

- Drink eight glasses of water a day. Water relieves stress. A de-hydrated body will succumb to decision fatigue faster than you can say, "Rightsize!"
- Get a good night's sleep. The body is a machine, and its functions are impaired when rest is inadequate.
- Eat healthy, fresh food, including vegetables and fruits. Avoid processed food, sugary treats, and soda. Expect to lose a few pounds during this process. How's that for an unexpected bonus?
- Get a little exercise. I didn't say run a marathon, did I? No, just walk for ten minutes a day. If you have a dog, Fido will think you're king of the pack. (OK, he already does, but now you'll be even more popular.)

That's my list. Embrace them all, or try one or two on for size. And remember that these are suggestions to help you, not to beat yourself up over. "Regina told me to do these things, and I didn't, so I am a bad person who will have a difficult move!" We aren't going to go there, OK? It's the last reaction Regina has in mind. Guilt, fear, and shame do not exist in the land of Zen Organizing.

If you never drink water, try consuming one sixteen-ounce bottle per day as a start. Keep the bottle with you and sip periodically. Rather than purchasing bottled water, you can get a cold-water thermos and a Brita pitcher and save a bundle. I sprinkle in some vitamin C crystals from Trader Joe's for an extra immune boost on demanding days to give plain water some spark and help my body stay healthy. If store-bought water is easier for you, please be sure to read the label and get fresh spring water, not tap water treated by the company. Hate the taste of water? (People actually say that to me, so I presume they have company out there.) Try fresh slices of lemon or lime. Heat the water and have lemon tea all day. This drink is a liver cleanser and helps restore your system's natural pH. How's that for a bonus? Or you could steep some fresh ginger and have a tea that improves digestion and reduces inflammation in the body. There are numerous benefits you won't find with soda. Where there's a will there's a way. Please don't drink those sugar-laden waters that are like consuming a liquid candy bar! Sugar gives you a rush of energy, and then your blood sugar plummets—along with your so-called energy. It's not uncommon to feel depressed after the inevitable crash. You'll also experience this nosedive with so-called energy drinks. As a species we humans seem to relish a temporary high rather than seeking a steady flow of good energy. What's that you say? You're a diet soda devotee? Drink that instead of water, and you may face dehydration and that guarantees fuzzy thinking and exhaustion. There's no substitute for water. I want you energized, not slumped on the sofa wailing, "I'm never gonna get out of here."

If you are mostly sedentary, try walking around the block. If your diet consists of steak and Twinkies, introduce yourself to vegetables and fruit one at a time. Forget that they are good for you, will keep you regular, and in some instances protect you from cancer. They even taste good! Remember, it takes twenty-one days of repeating an action before it becomes a habit. Do as much as you can each day and focus on your successes.

Making a Move Notebook

To make your move as organized and stress-free as possible, create a move notebook so that all of your planning notes are in one place. You can be making notes as you read this book. You can create an e-notebook using Google Docs, Microsoft One Note, Evernote, or the organizing tool you prefer. Most can be set up as private and locked, or you can make the notebook accessible to others in the family unit. Let's say you're out shopping and remember you need to stop at the paint store. If your partner has access to your move notebook, you may discover that item has been checked off as done. Partnership certainly makes a move less daunting. If you prefer a binder, use sheet protectors for those items that you need for reference but won't be writing on—for example, the contract with your mover or the rental receipts for your truck and dollies should you be doing your own move. If you are afraid you may lose these documents, for safety's sake, scan them into your computer. As you might imagine, there are apps for that. I use Genius Scan. You can also purchase a few heavy-duty poly file folders. They can take a lot of wear and tear. Now all these valuable documents can live in your file cabinet. There are many ways to solve organizing issues, and that is why it's such a creative endeavor.

To facilitate the creation of your move notebook, you'll find the weekly summary lists waiting for you online at ReginaLeeds.com. I've created a page you can easily and instantly copy, paste, and tailor to suit your needs. Most of us work digitally now, and this simple copy-and-paste will get your move notebook started.

By the way, all the organizing tools I mention in this book are featured on a special board I created at Pinterest.com (visit my various boards at http://www.pinterest.com/zenorg1). You can show your local store exactly what tool you are looking for when you go shopping. If you wish to order online, links are provided. Over time I'll add products and tips that I think will make your move a bit easier.

A Tidy Tool: Categorized Moving Files

You don't want piles of moving brochures and scribbled notes spreading out around the house like a fungus. I would divide the material by category and create a few files. This is especially necessary if you purchased a new home and you're also collecting decorating tips for that space. Use individual file folders for your categories and then store them all in your filing cabinet using box-bottom hanging file folders no wider than two inches. Conversely, if you want this material to be portable, try an expanding file holder or a portable file box. At Pinterest I have photos of all the products I'm suggesting as well as links to stores that sell them. If you have no clue what a portable file box is, for example, the visual is waiting for you.

These are all garden-variety supplies available at your local office-supply store or on the Internet. Any files you create in real time will likely have counterparts with similar material collected in folders on your computer. Be sure you use the same names for every type of folder, whether it's saved on your computer or in your filing cabinet. You need to keep those names consistent. Where you keep the information is not important, but your ease in finding it all is everything. For some reason people have flights of fancy and get creative on the fly. Be creative the first time you choose a name, and then be consistent; otherwise you may wind up wasting time searching for information, asking, "What the heck did I call that folder?" You don't have time to waste before a move! By the way, it would behoove you to empty your purse or briefcase each evening of any material you have gathered related to your move. A category is as strong as the items that compose it, and if the parts are scattered, you run the risk of a great piece of information slipping through the cracks.

The "B Word": Making a Budget

No, I'm not talking about female dogs. The "B word" that concerns me is "budget." Moving is expensive, and you need to factor in as many details as possible so you aren't blindsided. The most common refrain I hear from my clients on moving day is, "Regina, I'm bleed-ing money." Let's put a tourniquet on that wound and see instead how you can economize. First, we need to know what you have and how much you need to spend. A personal budget is really a neces-sity. Many people view a budget as a straightjacket that will not per-mit them to have any fun. Nothing could be further from the truth. Numbers are your friends because they never lie. Everyone needs a budget to get a monthly snapshot of his or her financial health. With any luck you'll have extra cash each month to save or invest. It's a financial tool you don't want to live without!

To create a budget, grab a pad of paper or fire up the computer. Draw a line down the center of a page or work in Excel. In the left column, make a list of all sources of income in a month. Next, in the right, make a list of all your monthly expenses: mortgage or rent, utilities and other bills, groceries costs, and so forth. (If you have periodic bills, factor in the percentage of that total amount you need to set aside each month. This way you won't be having convulsions when that yearly insurance premium comes due for your home or you get the bill for your semiannual union dues.) Now add up both columns and see where you are. In the best of all possible worlds, you have money left over each month for an emergency fund, long-term investing, and big-ticket items—you know, like this move. If you freelance like I do, your expenses are probably fairly static, but working with income when it fluctuates can be a challenge. Freelanc-ers can use their average income against their set expenses.

If you have a shortfall, you'll have to figure out what the move is going to cost and then decide how you'll raise that money. This might be just the incentive you need to sell some possessions that you no longer use. Perhaps you have to eliminate some expenses or reduce others. Call your cable company, cellphone carrier, and other service providers and see if you can cut your bills if only for six months. Give your credit card companies a call and see if you qualify for an interest-rate reduction. Paying bills on time puts you in the best position to receive these favors. It also boosts your FICO (credit) score, and that will come in handy if you have to move yourself. Big-ticket items, like truck rentals, will cost less if your credit score is high. If you are the unemployed partner in the relationship, it might be time to get a part-time job. If you have relatives in a position to help, see if you can float a no- or low-interest loan. Just remember it has to be paid back, so what you're buying is time.

Considerations for Moving to an Address to Be Determined

Though it's not ideal, sometimes you've got to plan a move before you even know where you're moving to. I've been there! Through circumstances beyond my control, I had to give notice at my last apartment before I found a new one. This situation really lights a fire under you in terms of organization. If you want to move in eight weeks but haven't as yet chosen your new location, here are some items to tackle this week:

- Once you know your budget and how much you can spend on the move, you can decide if you are paying too much for your current rental or can afford to move up in the world. This financial reality check will dictate where you look for your next home.

- In large cities agencies will help you find your ideal abode for a fee. You can also check Craigslist.org for ads or search popular real estate sites, like Zillow.com and Trulia.com.

- If you have time, walk or drive around your desired neighborhood looking for rentals. Not everyone registers with a service or advertises online.

- Walk into real estate offices and introduce yourself. Agents may have properties in escrow that happen to have your ideal guesthouse.

- Send out an e-mail blast or contact friends on your favorite social media sites. Personal networking can yield leads that are being held close to the vest.

THINGS TO DO WHEN MOVING OUT

- Check your current lease to see how much notice you need to give the management. You want to play by the rules and get your security deposit back, right?

- Have you painted any walls? You may be responsible for returning them to the original color before you go. In addition, leave the apartment in tidy condition if you have your eye on that deposit.

- Has Fifi or Fido done any damage? You'll need to repair that as well, especially if you handed over a pet deposit.

- Once your ducks are in a row, schedule a walk-through with the manager or owner. You are responsible for damage, not normal wear and tear. Each state has laws that dictate the amount of time the landlord has to return your deposit. Note that date on your calendar, and be sure you've received a check or an accounting for the use of those funds.

- Find out from management at both ends if you need to reserve a parking spot (or two) for your truck. Some neighborhoods require that moving trucks have a special parking permit. Call the local chamber of commerce or check out the city government website. You don't need a parking ticket on moving day; nor do you want to get off on the wrong foot with your new neighbors or leave a bad taste in the mouths of your old ones.

- What day are you planning to move? Are there elevator restrictions? Find out in advance because everything that slows the process down costs you money. Time really is money on moving day. You want to eliminate any delays and tell your mover about any restrictions at either location.

Box It Up!

Everyone who is moving requires boxes, so this week, do some re-search to figure out where you'll get yours and exactly what as-sortment you need. If you're doing your own move, you can ask for advice at a box store or interview a mover to get some guid-ance. In addition, Moving.com and ApartmentGuide.com provide a calculator that helps you estimate how many boxes you need and what types based on factors like how long have you been at your residence, how many people are moving, how many rooms you are packing up, and a general description of your stuff. You'll find boxes designed to handle basic household possessions. For exam-ple, wardrobe boxes transport hanging clothes; small file-size boxes are great for books and paper; large, deep boxes, called "dish packs," are designed for kitchen items.

Buying new boxes can be expensive, but many people prefer to do so because no one has ever used them before. The choice is yours. There are ways to save and even score free boxes, so let's take a look at your options:

- Get used boxes from your mover. They will be in great shape but sold at a discount. Many movers will come and pick them up when you're done. (Most will require you to have them cut down and tied together for pickup.) Your mover will be able to guesstimate how many boxes you need by surveying the pos-sessions you plan to take with you.

- Check on websites like Craigslist.org or Freecycle.org to see if anyone has just moved or is about to and will give you their unpacked boxes.

- If you're doing a "down and dirty" move on the fly, go to your local liquor store and ask for empty boxes. Those boxes trans-port liquid and glass, so you know they're sturdy.

- Drive around your neighborhood over the weekend, and see if you can spot someone moving in; maybe you can strike a deal for his or her boxes. Most people aren't in the mood to sell; they just want the empty boxes gone ASAP. I don't mean that you should drive around for hours trolling your hood! On the way to the grocery store or on the way home from soccer practice, cruise a few extra streets and check out the landscape.

- If you've been dealing with real estate agents, ask them if they have any clients with a move on the horizon who would give you their boxes once they've unpacked.

- Put the word out to family, friends, and social media contacts. Someone may know someone who is moving, and by day's end you could be hooked up.

- If you are a union member, you'll be able to score a discount on boxes. In fact, check with your representative because certain large moving companies offer discounts on supplies and the actual move to union members.

Remember my friend Carla from the introduction? She put the word out in an e-mail blast, and a former client who owns a box company agreed to donate whatever moving supplies she needs, and a Boy Scout troop volunteered to help pack. Miracles happen when you ask. Nothing happens if you do nothing but fret.

Two great aids for anyone contemplating a move are the popular websites Moving.com and ApartmentGuide.com. They have calculators for things like the number of boxes needed should you elect to do your own move. They can also assist you with details like mail forwarding. When I signed up, I received discount coupons for popular stores in my new neighborhood, like Pottery Barn and West Elm. If you aren't comfortable giving out personal information online, simply peruse the sites for items like the free calculators.

Finding the Mover of Your Dreams

The next big task is choosing a mover. Heaven knows they are not all created equal. Let's examine some things you'll want to know if you are securing bids. In this first planning week, you'll want to call a few potential movers. A little detective work will yield the names of reputable companies. When you call, ask the receptionist if the company services the area you're going to and if the desired date is available. If so, schedule a meeting for week two to go over the details of your move with a company representative. You don't have to inundate the person who answers the phone; just be prepared for the meeting with the rep. Schedule meetings with three to five companies, and see who offers the best deal and with whom you feel the most comfortable.

You want to prepare to meet with the moving companies the way you would for any critical meeting. This week, get your planning done; then next week you'll only need your notes.

(Next week, we'll examine what you need to get if you and your buddies are doing the move without the help of professional movers; see pages 50–52. Moving yourself is my least favorite option. People become pros at something and get paid top dollar for a reason. But if you're determined not to hire out, I've got direction for you in week two. Don't skip ahead, however, as you might need one or two of the pearls of wisdom I am about to drop here!)

Needless to say, the best mover is the one you have used before and had a good experience with or who has satisfactorily moved a trusted friend or family member. Under those circumstances, you don't need to know too much more than the price and whether the company is free the day you need it. Wintertime is slow for movers, and you should have no problem. Spring, summer, and early fall can be tricky, however. Eight weeks is more than enough time to reserve your desired slot. This is one step you can't afford to put off.

Following are some questions to help you find the right mover. Bear in mind that fees vary, so, once again, it's critical you know what you can afford. Using a credit card when it will be months or years before you pay it off makes your move many times more expensive than the quoted price and certainly more expensive than its worth. Make a note in your moving notebook of the questions below that pertain to your move. That way, you'll be prepared for your meeting with the moving company representative next week.

Along with pricing, you want to know as much about your mover and his practices as possible, and he needs to know specific details about your move. He'll need to eyeball what you intend to take with you. He'll ask about access at your current residence and at your destination. Unfavorable conditions can add time to the move, and he needs to factor in everything he can so that his estimate is accurate.

- Ask how long the company has been in business. Check its rating with the Better Business Bureau and online reviews, if they exist, at sites like Yelp.com. If you see nothing but bad reviews, take a pass, but also remember that any business will get a bad review from time to time. Some people just don't want to have a good outcome, do they? I weigh a bad review against the literacy of the person writing it and make my own judgment. If you are flying blind in your choices with no personal recommendations, check out not only the Better Business Bureau but also consumer-advocacy sites like MovingScam.com.

- Ask how you must pay for the move as few movers will take a personal check unless you have a long history with them. A surgeon client of mine was literally pulled out of the operating room when the truck arrived at the assisted-living facility he had chosen for his mother, and the driver would not accept the good doctor's personal check. The driver parked the semi and refused to unload the contents until he was paid either with a cashier's check or cash or received word from his boss that another form of payment was acceptable—and I was powerless to help. I never have close to $2,000 in cash in my purse.

- If you don't want to pack yourself, ask about packing services. You can save time and money over the course of the weeks before your move by packing the unbreakable items in your home, including books, linens, clothing, stuffed animals, boxed games, and pots and pans. Your professional packers will generally pack up the home the day before they load the truck. Doing both on the same day is a Herculean, time-consuming task, and it's rarely booked that way. Good movers pack all day long, and I would encourage you to let them do your breakables. (In chapter 2 I provide some tips for packing fragile items if you need to save money or feel more secure doing the packing yourself; see pages 76–78. Some websites give demonstrations of packing techniques. Try a Google search to start; then go to About.com, eHow.com, and YouTube.com.) Your mover may mention that the company offers unpacking as well as packing services. Please know that movers are not professional organizers. They unpack but create no order. You are free of boxes but still have a sea of stuff to deal with, so I suggest you decline.

- The representative may offer you insurance coverage. Know that if you have homeowners insurance, your goods are covered on the truck. Let your insurance provider know about the move and give them your new address as soon as you have it. Also ask your insurance provider how coverage for damage will be handled if the break is in a box you packed rather than one the movers did. (Yes, there's a difference in coverage.) And let your mover know you won't need to purchase his coverage. Such coverage is useful if you are doing a long-distance move and/or don't have a homeowner's insurance policy, but a reputable, experienced mover rarely has an issue on short hauls. Insurance is a nice moneymaker for them.

- When you have your estimates, compare not only the dollar amount but also the weight it is based on. This way you'll be sure all of them have a clear idea of the scope of the job. If you add significant items to be loaded onto the truck on the day of the move, your moving supervisor has the right to say you have nullified the estimate. You'll be renegotiating before he loads the truck, not after!

- If your move is going across town, find out if they intend to pack one day and move the next, as is the norm. If boxes and furniture are transferred at the mover's home base to another truck, you run the risk of breakage or theft. This is rarely done for a short haul, but it becomes a big issue with long-distance moves. For a long distance move, ask if the driver who picks up your load will be the one who drops it off. Get the facts so that you won't be startled to find that Manny, Moe, and Jack have been replaced by Tweedledum and Tweedledee, who have their own rig, meaning that your stuff has been moved an extra time.

- All the movers you interview should offer you the booklet *Your Rights and Responsibilities When You Move*. It's loaded with valuable information, so make a point to peruse it. If you aren't going to interview movers, you can still download a copy from the Federal Motor Carrier Safety Administration (FMCSA) website (https://www.protectyourmove.gov/consumer/awareness/rights/rights.htm).

- If you're moving between states, check to determine whether the interstate mover is registered with the FMCSA and has a US Department of Transportation number.

- Does your mover have the licenses and insurance coverage he needs to do business? Check the company out at SaferSys.org or call FMCSA to get information on the status of a company's licensing (202-366-9805) and insurance (202-385-2423).

- Ask if your crew will be regular company employees or guys who work on an as-needed basis. An established crew will be your best and most experienced bet.

- Ask each company representative how the movers will protect your home during the move. See if one is more conscious, for example, of protecting the wood floors or has a ready response about transporting delicate items like computers, TVs, or a piano.

You can learn a lot about skill level and experience from these responses.

- Ask if the company will move your plants and how. Moving is traumatic for all living beings, even plants. Most plants have trouble getting across town, let alone spending several days on a truck. You may want to give your leafy friends to others. If they are indeed going with you, and you'd like them repotted before the big day, check with your local nursery about when that should take place. Some species are more temperamental than others. Ask any ficus owner who has made a move with one!

- Finally, movers very often don't take cleaning products and other supplies you typically find in a garage. Find out now so you can make a plan should you wish to transport them. You don't want any surprises on the big day. If items need to be disposed of, you'll want to do that responsibly rather than simply leaving them for the next occupant.

The driver very often owns the rig and supervises the crew. You want to tip everybody who does a good job, especially the driver. He's the caretaker of your things, and if he's happy they will be safer. Tips, by the way, should be given in cash. If you add the amount to the total invoice, the company may not give it to the crew. And you do want to reward a good crew. Let them know you intend to do just that because it's very motivating. How much is appropriate? There is no standard as a tip is based on your opinion of the service and the complexity of the move. Did it involve transport across state lines? Did the driver have the rig overnight? Do you have expensive furniture and artwork that had to be handled with special care? In general the worker bees get a little less than the supervisor. If you are unsure, you can discuss tipping with the moving company representative when you have your meeting. By the way, your tip is based on the man-hours spent during the actual move, not on purchases like boxes, insurance, and packing materials.

You want to choose your mover carefully and have a seamless experience. Professional movers are, for the most part, skilled at packing and moving goods. If you go with a cut-rate, fly-by-night group, you'll get what you pay for. No matter how responsible the worker bees are, they are human, and accidents happen. So ask each representative about the following:

- If damages occur, what is the mover's responsibility?
- Does the company have a dispute settlement program?
- How will the movers handle "packed-by-owner" boxes? (Check with your homeowner's policy to see what your coverage is.)

If a representative answers straightforwardly, you're probably in the hands of a pro. If you get a vague response, think twice about booking the company no matter how much cheaper its estimate. Make sure you check with the Better Business Bureau.

It's a good idea to examine your furniture for any dings or marks that currently exist. You probably have them but don't see them. Photograph all preexisting damage so there's no question at the other end. Be sure you point these out to the moving company so that the team is aware of any existing issues. You don't want to blame a company for something that Uncle Charlie did five summers ago.

A good mover will put some type of covering on the floor to protect it. Be sure you let him know what type of floor he will encounter in the new space (there's a big difference between hardwood and carpet).

The mover will ask about the entry to the new home. Elevators add time, especially on a weekend when other tenants are home and need to go up and down. This is a real time suck in a city highrise, although that type of building generally has freight elevators reserved for these purposes. Stairs also add time and difficulty. If your entrance poses a challenge to the movers, expect to pay more. I once watched a mover strap a refrigerator to his back and take it up two flights of stairs in a New York City building. Whatever he got paid, it wasn't enough.

If you like the representative the moving company sends to your home, you'll probably like the crew. He's the front man, so he's usually chosen carefully. He may even be the owner. This rep can look at your stuff and know how many boxes you need and what type. Once you decide on his company, those boxes will be delivered to you. If you get your questions in order, this meeting will run smoothly, and you'll be in a position to compare the companies you interview based on their representatives' responses. The movers will be impressed with your level of organization and attention to detail. They'll also know you understand the ins and outs of this complicated and emotional undertaking.

GORILLA MOVERS AT YOUR SERVICE

I'd been assisting clients for over twenty-five years and felt certain I had experienced every possible snafu a move could bring until a few weeks ago. A young couple moved into my building with a baby and two small dogs. The moving truck was delayed leaving the East Coast and arrived a week late. We're a small building with a strong community. We all pitched in and came up with inflatable beds, a table and two chairs, and a few other basics. The day the truck arrived, every stick of furniture was broken or damaged. Items were smashed in boxes for the simple reason that they were packed hurriedly and without skill. The load had been left in storage for a few months, increasing the number of people handling the items. It ranks as the worst move I've ever witnessed. If you think my list of questions is too far-reaching, I invite you to remember my new friends and their gorilla move. I call it that because it appeared gorillas from the local zoo had been in charge.

A wonderful organization called the Delancy Street Foundation trains recovering substance abusers, ex-convicts, homeless individuals, and others who have hit rock bottom in new careers, including as professional movers. I had the privilege of unpacking clients recently who used Delancy Street Movers, and the work was top-notch. They have branches across the country; should you have one nearby, I highly recommend that you include them in the list of movers you contact. The fee you pay goes to the foundation, making your entire expense (less product purchases like boxes and packing material) tax deductible. It's win-win from every possible angle. I will be using them on my next move and recommend them to all my clients.

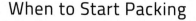

When to Start Packing

Leaving my last apartment was a very emotional experience because of the length of time I had been there and the life experiences that I'd had within those walls. It wasn't just an apartment to me; it was my home. I asked for (used) boxes a full two months before the big day and started packing immediately. Once the first box was full and sealed, the move was real, and I had passed the point of no return. After that, packing up was easier than if I had waited until the week before.

You have to choose carefully what you pack weeks before the move. Starting next week, our major work will be rightsizing the individual rooms in your home in preparation for moving and packing. You need to decide when is the best time to start packing for your particular situation and the number and ages of the people involved. If you can afford it, the movers can pack everything for you. (The more they pack the more it costs, but if you have the funds or are being moved by a corporation that is picking up the tab, this is the best solution.) You can live in your home pretty much as is right up to the day of the move. If you have a big family and young children, you will find that too many packed boxes upset the equilibrium in the home. Even pets become stressed as the signs of an impending move make their appearance. It's a delicate balancing act. The key question is where to put the packed boxes.

I give packing tips with each chapter after I help you divest the room in question of the items you don't need to take with you, but depending upon your situation, you may not pack those items that week. You can delay the packing, but three weeks from the move date would be the biggest delay I'd entertain.

I began boxing items before my recent move at a very early stage because I am self-employed and worried that a sudden influx of client work would prevent me from having the energy or time to pack. It was easier to live with tidy stacks of boxes than to take the chance I'd wind up paying more because the movers had to do all the work. Even if money is no object, you can save a few bucks and put unbreakable items into boxes.

Fresh Eyes Exercise

To prepare you to rightsize your home in the weeks ahead, do the "fresh eyes exercise" in this planning week. I'd like you to leave the house and run an errand or take the dog for a walk, or perhaps do this when you return from work. Pretend you have never been in this home before and have no clue who lives here.

Quietly walk from room to room making mental notes. Are the occupants tidy, messy, or simply overrun with stuff? Do items jump out at you as superfluous? I went into a home once and discovered two large dining room tables. One was in use, and the other had become a catchall because the owner felt that one day he might need it, but he really had no practical use for it. I suggested he donate it to a local charity. He'd have a tax deduction, a family would get an affordable dining room table, and he could enjoy the free space. Never think of free space as empty. It's a form of visual quiet. Enjoy it rather than rushing to fill it.

Peer into cupboards. Look inside drawers. Peek into closets. Don't ignore the pantry! And please look at the garage. In most cases a home can be neat as a pin, and the garage looks like a dumpsite. After the tour, sit down and either make literal notes or do a little mental housekeeping before you commit details to paper or a word document. What do you think? Keep in mind that you are going to pay to transport your stuff, so it should have actual or emotional value.

Here are some items that you can definitely get rid of in the weeks to come. Make a note in your move notebook if it'll help you to remember later.

- Ancient tax records that the Internal Revenue Service is never going to want to see. (Do save the return forever.) Visit http://www.irs.gov/Businesses/Small-Businesses-&-Self-Employed/How-long-should-I-keep-records for specific instructions.

- Broken kitchen equipment that you hope to fix one day. You've been saying that for years. Get real.

- Office equipment that's no longer used or needed. You save it because you "paid good money for it." It's collecting dust, and someone else could make excellent use of it.

- Clothing you haven't worn or that hasn't fit for ages. If you lose weight, you won't want your reward to be a wardrobe from twenty years ago.

- Clothing that's frayed, torn, or missing a button or snap, shoes so worn that even an expert cobbler would weep if he saw them, and deceased relatives' clothes that you never wear but keep for sentimental reasons.

- Toys the kids outgrew years ago.
- Cheap vases that came with a flower delivery.
- Extra dish sets that you never use, but again sentiment urges you to hang on.
- Magazines that you intend to read because you just know there's an article of interest in at least one of them.
- Catalogs that come every month.
- The newspapers stacking up because you are certain there are words of wisdom in there and, after all, you "paid good money," so you don't want to be wasteful.
- Expired medications. (Don't pour them down the drain or flush them because you will be adding meds to the water supply.) Your pharmacy may take them back for disposal, or you can buy a mailer at your drugstore that is designed for this purpose. The medications go to an official location for destruction. (In a pinch you can just put them in a plastic bag with some coffee grounds and hammer them into a fine powder. In that state they can be tossed; however, be certain the package is sealed because you don't want to poison any local creatures like dogs, cats, or birds.)
- Expired food (this includes frozen items, which in general last no more than six months).
- A superabundance of coffee mugs.
- Expired self-care products like body lotions, makeup, and mouthwash.
- Sports equipment from that long-ago five minutes when you wanted to start skiing, horseback riding, or playing hockey. And how about the Nordic Track that's eaten all the space in the guest room? You used it once, and now it's a monument to good intentions.

By now you get the idea. You may have one or many or all of these things. This stuff needs to go. It needs to exit your life long before the moving truck arrives. Do not pretend that you will go through it at the other end. If you were truly interested, you would have done so long ago. The reality is that some of us find stuff comforting. Extra weight and excess stuff frequently mask emotional pain.

A Quickie to End the Week

I certainly don't expect you to tear through all the items listed above this week! I want you to start with one item or one category, like all the broken kitchen equipment, and get it out of the house. And I mean literally out of the house—off the property and into its new home. There is no point in piling it up by the front door and letting it sit there for the next several weeks. Putting it in the trash can tonight and taking it back out again in the morning before the garbage truck arrives is an exercise in futility.

This first purge will be like the first domino: once it's pushed, momentum will take you toward the finish line. I address everything from broken kitchen equipment to ancient tax records in later chapters, dealing with tasks that seem insurmountable in detail. Getting stuff out will give you a sense of accomplishment, shift the energy in the home, and build momentum. A trick to help you is to use a timer. Give yourself no more than eight minutes in any one space this week to grab a few items that you know you can get rid of without remorse. "Trust me" is a dangerous phrase, but I have to ask you to do just that and to remember that I've been doing this for over twenty-five years. I don't just think there's power in elimination; I've learned it through experience.

I've given you a lot to do this week, but have you noticed it's almost all mental work? You sit at a desk to craft a budget, establish your agenda for the upcoming mover meetings, and make phone calls to schedule them. These tasks will give you a firm foundation for the process to come, but it's best if you do something physical as well.

Everyone has at least one item he knows he doesn't need. Usually it's way more than one, but let's be conservative this week. Pulling out that first item is very often like breaking the glue that keeps you stuck in the status quo. My friend Carla will receive an item and never let it go. This would be less problematic if she lived in Buckingham Palace, where she'd have access to over one hundred rooms. For mere mortals, however, stuff has to leave at some point, or else you're living in a private landfill or cemetery. Neither is a cheery image.

Week's Summary

- ❏ Create a move notebook and easy filing system for the notes and materials you'll amass over the weeks.
- ❏ Create or adjust your family budget so you know exactly what you can afford in terms of your move.
- ❏ Research sources for moving boxes.
- ❏ A little detective work will yield the names of reputable movers. Schedule meetings with three to five, and see who offers the best deal and with whom you feel the most comfortable.
- ❏ Do the "fresh eyes exercise."
- ❏ Eliminate one difficult item or category from your home to release stuck energy.

A Closing Thought

This week you move from "Gosh! I need to move" to "I'm moving in eight weeks and I've started to craft a plan that will save me time, money, and energy." I think a simple but refreshing reward would be a nice hot bath. Toss some Epsom salts into the tub and relax those tense shoulder and tired leg muscles. You've laid the foundation. Congratulations!

TAKE THE FIRST STEPS

Understand that
you own nothing,
Everything that
surrounds you
is temporary,
only the love in your heart will
last forever.

—ANONYMOUS

I HOPE THE QUOTE THAT OPENS THIS CHAPTER PROVIDES YOU with some comfort—or at least a little perspective. This week will find you having the all-important mover meetings, and hopefully by the end of the week, you'll have your big day booked. Remember, you can schedule a few meetings even if you don't intend to use a mover. They usually have moving literature you may find interesting, and they may have some tips to share. And who knows? You might be so enamored with the representative that you decide to hire the company! Whether you hire a mover or decide to go it alone, you can rest easy knowing that the most expensive decision has been made, and you've chosen someone you can afford and trust.

It's important to know what stays and what goes. It's equally important to decide where the exiting items are going to land and to make those preparations as early as possible. The start of week eight is not the time to find out your sister-in-law does not in fact want your couch and neither do any local charities. In addition to thinking about "stuff disposition," this week we get to work on the kitchen. The heart of the home is very often a burial ground for obsolete items like broken equipment we've intended to have repaired for years, inherited items we hold on to out of guilt, and items we have outgrown (sippy cups, anyone?). We'll clear out the excess, think about the next kitchen, and tackle the sister room to the kitchen—the all-important laundry room.

Mover Meetings

In week one, you'll have scheduled meetings with a few movers. When they come to your home this week, have your moving notebook with your prepared questions at the ready (see pages 32–37). The more prepared you are, the faster and more productive the meetings will be.

You want to have a clear sense of which pieces of furniture are going and which will be donated or given away. I have to stress that changing your mind about a lamp is no big deal, but suddenly deciding to take your double-door subzero refrigerator, which took three men to deliver and place, may affect your estimate. After all, big-ticket items require extra time and care to transport. They also take up room on the truck, and if you are crossing state lines and other families are scheduled to share the space, there could be a last-minute snafu. Your preparation eliminates drama on moving day. And on that day, more than most, time really is money.

One of my clients booked his move and was given a guaranteed estimate. He subsequently decided to move to a different location and forgot to tell the movers they were going eight miles rather than two within the city limits. The move fell on a Saturday, when traffic is lighter, and during a holiday weekend, so my client thought there would be no problem. The owner of the company freaked when he heard the news at the end of day one, and on day two my client had three men instead of four, and they were told to haul you-know-what and not go over the estimate. My client was happy to pay any additional charges, but the movers had their orders and cut corners. Let's just say that the wood furniture did not arrive in pristine condition, and it cost $500 to have a wood specialist come out and remove the scratches.

If your move is during the high season, you want to choose your mover this week and book as soon as possible. The company will take care of all the paperwork once it receives your order. In fact it will soon deliver boxes, labels, and tape. My mover sent all the necessary paperwork in a PDF file, and we each signed using DocuSign. No matter how it happens, once you choose a mover, you'll need the following key documents safely tucked into your move notebook:

- Estimate
- Bill of lading (sometimes combined with the estimate)
- Inventory (generated on moving day)

The ideal estimate is either binding or guaranteed not to exceed a certain amount. Both put a cap on what your move will cost. Interstate moves are based on weight and distance. Intrastate moves are governed by state laws. California, for example, requires your mover to give you a binding estimate, whereas other states forbid a mover from doing so. You'll need to check local regulations. The big variables governing the estimate are time and weight if you are leaving the state. You have a lot of control over both. That's why we're devoting time each week to eliminating items you don't need to schlep to the new home. If you are unsure about any of the details from your meetings, call the mover for additional information or clarification. And don't assume that the company with the lowest bid is the best. If three movers have roughly the same estimate, how exactly did the fourth cut expenses? You aren't shopping for a new best friend, so don't be afraid to question any detail, and don't be shy about negotiating a better price. You may not be successful, but it might pay to ask.

When You Should Definitely Hire Professional Movers

If you have expensive artwork, it will need to be professionally crated. I'd use the movers if only for that task. If you don't have a rider on your homeowners insurance for expensive possessions like jewelry and artwork, be sure you secure them now and let your insurance carrier know how you intend to have them transported. Imagine moving valuable artwork in the backseat of your car because you're just going across town, only to have it crushed by an air bag when you stop suddenly at an intersection. Good luck collecting full-market value on that claim.

Let's not forget the elephant in the room called a piano. If it's expensive, like a Steinway, you will need to use a professional mover. I had wealthy clients in New York who hired a moving company sight unseen on the recommendation of a neighbor. I was flown in to set up the household while they went off to the St. Regis to relax. The move was from one apartment to another in the same building. When the movers asked if I had newspaper because they forgot to bring any moving paper, I knew we were in trouble. One gentleman was still in street clothes from a long night of drinking. When the baby grand was lifted, I had to walk out of the room because I was certain that piano was doomed. We all survived. Ultimately they were asked to move only the large pieces. I personally moved every other item using one of those carts the bellboys have to transport your luggage inside a hotel. It took all night. That move was a *Saturday Night Live* skit, and I've never experienced its like again. The moral of the story: you should always meet someone from the company before you book.

You may also have to ship your vehicle. If your move is triggered by a new job or transfer to another area, your employer will most likely have a recommendation, as will your mover. I'd contact those references, but you can also use Google to find services in your area. As for your mover, you'll want to check the company's rating with the Better Business Bureau. You can work out a date for pickup that will have your vehicle in your new location at roughly the same time as your household goods. Time of year will have a direct effect on how busy the company is, as will the possibility of inclement weather. In general you want to make your reservation at least three weeks in advance. Once the car is loaded onto the transport truck, you should be able to track its movements as it makes its way to your new home.

A reliable company will, of course, carry insurance on the vehicle, but I would check with your own insurance provider to see if your carrier has any additional requirements. Remove all personal items from your vehicle. It isn't wise to load your car as a way to transport a few boxes. As a rule of thumb the company insures your vehicle during transport to the new location, but it will not be responsible for personal items inside the car. Once the car arrives safely, you'll have the fun of dealing with the local DMV. If you're a member, the

Auto Club of America may be able to assist you with most, if not all, of the details. You have auto registration to change as well as a new driver's license to secure. It might be a great time to join the Auto Club, and depending on your tax status and whether you claim any deductions, your membership may be a tax deduction. In large cities you may also have to contend with neighborhood parking regulations. In Los Angeles we have to register our vehicles once a year in order to street-park in our neighborhoods, secure guest passes if needed, and renew them throughout the year. You don't want a parking ticket, so be sure that someone—whether it's you or your virtual assistant (see below) or your savvy teenager—learns all the ins and outs of your new hood.

When You Are the Mover

If you are your own mover, you'll need to investigate rates for truck rentals and your friends' availability. You might even ask a local moving company if it uses any guys (or gals) who "job-in" on an as-needed basis and might want to work that day. It's a long shot, but at least you'd have some experienced hands on deck. Moving furniture is an art, and even the strongest of humans can ding, scratch, and break easily lifted items. In the world of moving, finesse can trump strength. Getting the refrigerator off the ground and onto a dolly is one thing; knowing how to maneuver it around corners, into an elevator, or down a flight of stairs is a horse of a totally different color. Choose wisely. I had a client, a movie producer, who would not hire professional movers no matter what I said. He went out and picked up day laborers waiting on a street corner for work. They were sweet men who knew zero about moving furniture, and we had a steep climb up to the entry. The adage "penny wise, pound foolish" comes to mind. It was a harrowing experience.

Do rent at least one, if not two, dollies for the big day. I'm not talking about that folding dolly you keep in the trunk of your car. I mean the kind a professional mover uses. Time is of the essence, and you want as many boxes as possible moving out of the house to the truck on every trip. Invest in special bags or the wraps movers use to protect furniture on the truck. Again, it's penny wise, pound foolish to scrimp on items that protect the investment you made in your furniture. Finally, let me say a word about the paper you use to

LIGHTEN THE LOAD: A VIRTUAL ASSISTANT

Right about now, your head is probably beginning to swim with details. This is the perfect time to introduce the notion of hiring a virtual assistant—a highly organized individual who enjoys doing the sort of research moving requires. For a fee he or she can take a lot off your plate. Your virtual assistant can present the research results you requested, which in turn makes the decision-making process for the myriad details of moving easier and faster. He or she can do things like schedule appointments, take care of address-change details, and have your utilities turned on in the new place and shut off in the old. It may cost you a few dollars, but you'll save time and energy and avoid stress. Interview a few candidates and be sure to choose someone who has helped with a move in the past. Online you can find numerous assistants at websites like oDesk.com or Elance.com. You can check with friends, put the word out at work, or google the phrase "virtual assistant" and add your area. I would ask for a resume and a list of happy clients. I'd also chat with at least two previous clients who needed the kind of help you are seeking. I would never give a stranger access to my credit cards, my bank account, or any other financial information. Take the time to find the most qualified, affordable, and easy-to-deal with assistant, and this may be the last research you do for a long time. Ask the person who prepares your taxes if this expense is tax deductible—potentially another bonus in addition to saved time and energy.

cushion the boxes. Many people use newspaper because it's cheap and plentiful, especially if you subscribe to a newspaper. But the ink on that paper is going to make everything filthy. The paper used by professional movers is expensive, but it's also worth its weight in gold. I would absolutely budget for it. Needless to say, you'll want a professional tape dispenser and several rolls of tape.

SELF-CARE TIP FOR THE WEEK

I HOPE BY NOW you're exercising, sleeping through the night, eating healthy meals, and drinking enough water. These are habits to embrace for life, but they are certainly critical aides in countering the avalanche of stress a move causes. This week I have another tip to add to your arsenal: destressing with a Bach flower remedy called Rescue Remedy. You can either put it under your tongue or use in that water you're drinking. It's available online at places like Amazon or at local health-food emporiums like Whole Foods and Sprouts.

Dr. Bach was an English physician and surgeon who discovered that certain flower essences had a remarkable ability to ease emotional stress in humans. Rescue Remedy's formula includes several of the main flower essences and is designed for high-stress or traumatic situations. It can't hurt. It isn't expensive. And it won't interfere with any medications you're taking. If Fido and Fifi are starting to get a bit naughty, put a few drops in their water. The whole family can guzzle it on moving day. OK, I'm kidding. No guzzling allowed!

Creating the New Space

This week you'll need to begin to craft a plan for the furniture, decorative items, collectibles, memorabilia, and general stuff that inhabits your physical space. If you are making a "lateral move," say from a two-bedroom, two-bath home to another of the same size, you have the easiest move of all. It's still good to decide if any pieces of furniture need to be replaced or if you have been given the perfect opportunity to shake things up a bit in terms of decor. I had clients who loved the colonial American look. Walking into their home was like stepping into eighteenth-century Boston or Williamsburg. They moved to an ultra modern home for extra space after the birth of their first child, and that decor was out of place. I saw that when they bought the house, but they didn't believe me—until they unpacked. Over time they needed to redecorate so that the furnishings matched the architecture of the house. Don't neglect that detail when you're house hunting.

Another couple moved the entire contents of their home from London to Los Angeles. As you might imagine, what works in an English town house won't work in sunny Southern California. The bulk of that furniture found its way to the garage and was ultimately sold. What a waste! Take everything into consideration as you plan. If you're going to ditch items, then donate them and get a tax deduction; don't pay to transport them to a new location and then make the donation. Let's craft a plan of attack so that you aren't left wandering from room to room overwhelmed and depressed.

Please don't think that I advocate tossing out all of your current furniture. In fact, as you go through your home, remember that paint can transform an outmoded table into a knock-out accent piece. You are also free to repurpose items. Who said an old dresser not needed in your bedroom can't become the repository for all of your office supplies? Or maybe that same dresser has such a deep top that it could function as a changing table in your new baby's room? Perhaps you are no longer interested in grandma's china, and it's going to one of your children, but you wonder what to do with the hutch where you have displayed it for the past twenty

INSPIRATION

Some people know their style inside out, while others get flummoxed by the very concept of design. If you have no ideas for how your new home can look, several websites are waiting to inspire you. Here are my favorites:

- Pinterest.com
- Houzz.com
- Instagram.com
- ClosetFactory.com

And don't forget the time-honored tradition of working with a professional designer. If you can't afford to have him or her design the entire house with you, schedule a few consultations and gather ideas. Many professional organizers, like myself, have been in and out of countless homes, and we too can offer some ideas. You can even glean some great ideas from a Feng Shui consultant.

At Pinterest.com you can create a free account and set up design-idea boards for every room in the house. You add images as you encounter them. It's the digital version of the scrapbook many of us grew up making, except it takes up no space and requires a lot less time. If you use a smart phone, you're taking those boards with you every time you shop. Please peruse the boards I have created for organizing (http://www .pinterest.com/zenorg1)!

For those who are more tactile, you can cut images out of magazines and do a mind map or dream board. You just need some poster board from an office-supply store and a glue stick. I'd make this board's images represent the feel for the home, while your Pinterest boards can reflect specific ideas for each room. Again, this is just a suggestion for those who are stuck as to how to personalize their space. In the end that's all the word "decorating" means, isn't it?

years? Why not use those now bare shelves for that growing collection of pottery? Or maybe you'll be using the dining room table for your craft projects, and the hutch will be the perfect place for craft supplies and completed photo albums or scrapbooks. Think outside the box before you off-load; that way, if you do decide to sell or donate, you won't have any regrets. You'll know for certain that you gave the dresser and all the other items thoughtful consideration before you sent them off to their new homes or even to the local consignment shop.

Stuff Disposition:
Strategies for Clearing Unneeded Items

When you walked through the house last week during the "fresh eyes exercise" (page 39), you no doubt looked at some items and realized you didn't need them in the new location. Perhaps the next home has less square footage or a different style of architecture or you're ready for a change. If these items won't fit in the trunk of your car, you may have to call someone to take them away. Depending on the quality of the item and the size of your city, you will no doubt have a selection of charities to choose from. Make a list of what you wish to give, take a photo of each item (to send to the charity if necessary, but certainly to keep as a record for taxes), and set aside some time this week to make calls or visit the charities' websites. Some people like chatting with real, live human beings; others just want to seal the deal. The choice is yours. Set a date for pickup.

If you know instantly that a particular item won't be coming with you, you don't need to spend any time with it. If it's going to a friend or relative, designate a forty-eight hour window for that person to come and get it. After that, the item is going to a charity and he or she can purchase it at the storefront. When your friend or relative has finished railing against you for being so heartless, simply say, "Thank you for sharing your feelings" and move on. Moving is tough, and you'll survive if you have to be as well.

By the way, if you are a parent to children who are long gone from the home but keep items stored in your attic or garage, the years of free storage are over. Let them be responsible for whatever they need to store. In addition, in every family there seems to be one person designated as the family member who keeps everything for everyone else. Once again, if you are a de facto storage facility for your siblings, aunts, uncles, and cousins, it's time to close shop and let all the "kids" take responsibility (even if those kids are in their fifties).

The Power of Fear

Now that you have identified those items you know in your heart need to go, you may be stymied by some entrenched fears. They tend to sound something like this:

- "I paid good money for that."
- "I might need it one day."
- "That belonged to my late (mother, father, best friend, mentor)."
- "I want to know the person who gets my . . . "
- "I bought that when I was (in college, at my first job, pregnant, living in New York), and I just can't part with it, even though I know I should."

Let's examine each of these rationales in turn. You may have some unique objection to parting with the crap—uh, stuff—you no longer need or want, but I think you'll share my vision after you read the following because letting go is the right thing to do.

PROMISE ME

One day toward the end of my mother's life, I came into the living room to find her crying. I was terrified and certain she was in pain. My mother had received a terminal diagnosis the year before. She told me as she looked around at all of her antiques that she knew they didn't mean anything to me and that after she died I would just toss them. I told her I would keep them. My mother made me promise that I would keep all of them forever. I was twenty-five, nursing a dying woman all by myself. I was exhausted, overwhelmed, and afraid. I promised. Who would do any different?

I've never calculated how much those antiques cost me in time, money, and energy over the years, but it was a small fortune. Five years after she passed, I moved the contents of the house, including those antiques, back to New York. The first calculation would be how expensive it was to maintain a house I didn't live in for five years but kept because it was my parents' last home. The next one would be that four-hundred-mile move back to New York from Pennsylvania. Within six months I decided to move to Los Angeles, and everything was moved across the country. I had to have an apartment big enough for Mom's antiques and furniture. You don't want to know how much that three-thousand-mile move cost. You catch my drift here, right? I know from personal experience that no deceased person has ever come back from the dead and asked about his or her belongings. I'm living proof that sometimes well-meaning heirs give their loyalty to stuff. Please don't make my mistake.

I have since given the furniture away. Some went to my best friend after her divorce; some I donated to charity. I sold the antiques to collectors delighted to have the pieces. I came to believe that each item had a life of its own and its visit with me had come to an end. It was time for others to use the furniture and for the antiques to grace other homes. Nothing is forever. Keeping items long past their usefulness or meaning is like locking someone away in a closet. They are in your home but not really welcome. They are prisoners. Let them go.

"I paid good money for that."

I have no doubt you did, but what is your point? If an item is no longer wanted or used, it should go. If it's tattered, torn, frayed, soiled, or in any other way not fit to see the light of day without someone wondering if you need a personal telethon, it should go. If it's so out of date that you would look absurd wearing it, let it go.

If you bought something expensive that has retained its value but that you no longer want, you might recoup some of your investment by selling it on eBay. If you don't have the time or the inclination for Internet sales, there are folks who do that for a living and take a commission. But you aren't limited to one moneymaking outlet. Do you work for a large corporation? Post the item on the company bulletin board. Don't forget your spiritual community board or the one for the sport you participate in. We're all hooked into groups of people or know others who are, so it's not impossible to get your item in front of hundreds, if not thousands, of people with a few computer keystrokes. I guarantee someone out there wants your item.

Selling items takes time you may not have. Consider the possibility of creative donating! I like to turn my clients on to little-known organizations dedicated to doing good with donated items. Planet Aid.org recycles textiles and supports international development projects around the world. The organization has yellow donation bins in most US cities and accepts clothing and shoes. Visit the website to see if what you have to give is a good match for the items Planet Aid seeks.

Another creative way to give some items a new life and purpose is to offer them to the local community theater. A vintage item no one will pay more than a few dollars for might just be the missing piece in a revival the theater plans. If you have warm coats you no longer wear, give them to a charity like New York Cares, which has a coat drive

A TIP FOR CONSIDERATE GIVING

Many people use a disaster like an earthquake, flood, or fire to donate items they have been keeping for sentimental reasons. Even if no tax deduction is involved, the act of making a donation raises their self-esteem. Please be realistic about the items you give. In the aftermath of Katrina, for example, no one needed wedding dresses, woolen slacks, or winter coats. Be sure the items you give will fulfill the intended purpose of helping those in need. Don't let their calamity be the impetus you need to clean out your closet. See the resources section for lots of ideas for creative ways to give considerately.

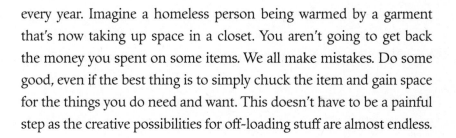

every year. Imagine a homeless person being warmed by a garment that's now taking up space in a closet. You aren't going to get back the money you spent on some items. We all make mistakes. Do some good, even if the best thing is to simply chuck the item and gain space for the things you do need and want. This doesn't have to be a painful step as the creative possibilities for off-loading stuff are almost endless.

"I might need it one day."

Yes, you might. You might also be hit by an asteroid, run over by a roll of industrial paper, rocket to the moon with Sir Richard Branson, or marry into royalty. The point is that "one day" is not likely to come, so holding on to an item you haven't touched for years is just pointless. If it's a piece of dated furniture that you think will fit in the new home, consider painting it a wild color and make it an accent piece. Or assign it a new use. Let's say you have a great old dresser, but it just won't fit in the new bedroom. What about putting it in a hallway near the bedroom and making it the repository for your linens? The foyer might be the place for it if you can store seasonal hats, gloves, and scarves in the drawers. On top you could place a basket for keys and maybe one for Fido's leash, harness, and poop bags. Or perhaps you could put it in a big kitchen and keep all the table linens in it? Exhaust your possibilities, and then think of doing something wonderful like donating it to a women's shelter. Women starting their lives over deserve lovely things, don't they? Beautiful possessions can raise our self-esteem. Your dresser, clothing, or old computer might help someone embark on a productive life. Isn't that more rewarding than letting an item take up space and collect dust in your home because you "might need it one day"?

The "I might need it one day" rationale very often reflects anxiety created by a traumatic experience. The Great Depression created a generation of fearful people. But an individual trauma can also be the culprit, and odds are that you've never connected the dots. See the box titled "Fire Storm" (below) for a story that exquisitely and simply describes this sort of unconscious wound and how it controls our lives. If you've suffered one of these, I hope the story opens doors of understanding for you.

FIRE STORM

I was invited to participate in a Los Angeles event hosted by a large corporation to honor some women executives. The company took over a private home, and every room held a surprise. You might get a mani-pedi, have your fortune told, or meet a Feng Shui master and me, the Zen Organizer. A woman would enter and tell us of some challenge in her life. I'd offer organizing tips to help remedy the situation, and the master would offer some tips from the Black Hat or Intuitive school of Feng Shui.

One of the first women to enter brought her two best buddies with her. They stood just behind her and mirrored her body language at every juncture. I thought of her as the General and her friends as the Lieutenants. Clearly their job was to support her, and her job was to angrily challenge us. "Well," she said, "I find the minute I get rid of something, I need it in about two weeks, so why should I bother?" I think I surprised her when I said, "Well, I don't think you should get rid of anything! You have what is known in metaphysics as a consciousness of loss. As long as you believe this to be true, it will play out over and over. So the moral of the story is that you should hold on to everything!" She relaxed a wee bit. "But what interests me," I added, "is where did this consciousness of loss come from: have you ever been robbed, lost your wallet, or had to move quickly?" She assured me that she had never suffered any kind of traumatic loss.

But when the Feng Shui master began his questions, slowly a story emerged. When she was five, she had gone on her first sleepover. She remembered packing her little overnight bag with great joy. While she was away, her older brother accidentally burned down the house! Everything was lost. The next day she had no home to return to. There it was, staring her in the face: a huge traumatic event involving loss, and yet she saw no connection. I asked gently if there might be a link between this horrible experience and her inability to toss anything for fear she would need it again. She said she had never thought about it but would look into the possibility.

When it's someone else's trauma, we very often see the connection immediately. If you can't let go of something because you might need it one day, ask yourself where that conviction came from. Is it a family belief? Did it originate with a trauma? Are you exactly like one of your parents? Identifying the source of the behavior or belief you wish to change will free you to put a new behavior or belief in its place. We live in a cause-and-effect universe. You'll never achieve a new effect by holding on to an old cause.

You may indeed give something away and later need it. If that happens, please just replace the item. Don't launch into a monologue of self-recrimination. It's either a fluke, or you made a mistake. When you're flying a fighter jet, a lapse in judgment can be catastrophic. When you give away a pair of snow boots, a bag of screws, or a hair dryer, the replacement cost is minimal. Try to see the reality of the situation and eighty-six the need to make yourself feel bad.

"That belonged to my late (mother, father, best friend, mentor, or someone else special to you)."

Ah, the power we invest in the possessions of the dead. I told you the story of my mother's things (see the "Promise Me" box on page 57). I could write an entire book about what happens to the belongings of the departed. Usually the pendulum swings from holding on to everything, like I did, to dumping it all without a look back. There has to be a middle ground, and that's what I'm suggesting you find. Here are some questions you might ask yourself to move the process along:

- How many items like the one I'm considering did the person leave?
- Can I choose one or two and then distribute the rest to other family members and friends?
- Did the deceased ever talk about his or her wishes for the item in question?
- Is there enough cash to pay any inheritance taxes due or to cover burial expenses? Will the sale of this item help?
- Do I have photos of the person wearing, using, or standing next to this item?
- Will my spouse, children, or others I'm living with like this item, or will it take up space and deprive them of the opportunity to express themselves? Not everyone enjoys living in a home crowded with the possessions of a long-dead relative. Are your spouse or children reflected in the furnishings, or are they visually dealing with your late mother 24/7?

You get the idea. I hope these questions open your mind to new ways of looking at the situation and to finding solutions you might not have considered. There are very creative ways to remember a person without turning your home into a museum. Of course, we want to honor the person in every way possible, and I'm not suggesting you begin divesting yourself the day after the funeral. Give yourself some time; just don't wait until you find yourself stuck. If you are moving right after the funeral, perhaps this is the one time downsizing can legitimately take place in the new home. And if you need to deal with the project the day after the funeral, consider calling in a company that handles estate sales. Get the help you need. The grieving period is no time to go it alone.

Here are a few creative ways to deal with your loved one's items:

- Create a shadow box or special album that holds not only images but also items like swatches of fabric or a lock of hair. You can bring a photo to life in this way. This can be a creative project with a result that many will enjoy for years.

- Do you need to give away someone's clothing? Consider taking a few buttons from each garment and make a piece of "button art." Or replace the ordinary buttons on a coat or jacket of yours with special ones from this person's clothing.

- Did you inherit a wedding dress? Very often today's bride wants to choose her own, but you can find a clever way to cherish grandma's dress. Take it to a skilled dressmaker and have it tailored into a fashionable cocktail dress. And yes, do have it dyed a festive color! I know a lovely artist named Carolyn Simon (CarolynSimonDesigns.com) who makes jewelry from wedding dress lace. Imagine wearing a piece of history every day rather than having a huge box in the attic containing a dress no one will wear or look at!

- Take the stones out of settings you don't like and have them reset in jewelry you design.

- If you have far-away relatives who want some huge item, like grandma's baby grand, but just don't know when they can pick it up, tell them you will send them the paperwork for a local storage unit. They can pay to have it transported and stored. You are not a public facility.

- Donate business suits to an organization like Dress for Success and help someone enter the professional workforce.
- Donate clothing and furniture to your favorite local charity or women's shelter.
- Find the right group for specialty items. For example, musical instruments would be appreciated by a high school band. One of my clients donated an antique piano to a Hollywood prop house.

Think outside the box so that the items once treasured by your loved one can have a new life with someone else. If some things truly need to be tossed, consider that the deceased was no doubt going to get around to that one summer afternoon. Tattoo these words on your heart: you will lose much if you keep too much.

"I want to know the person who gets my . . ."

I was stopped in my tracks the first time a client voiced concern that someone at the charity would keep her donation. My response to that sort of worry is, "So what?" You get the tax deduction, and in the end it doesn't matter who gets the item. You aren't going to use it, so what difference does it make? But if you must know who will be receiving your belonging, here are some ways to donate cleverly:

- Call your local house of worship and see if there's a family in need. Ask to be connected to them and make the delivery personally.
- Call your child's school to see if a family is in distress and proceed to make your direct donation. I bet the family that lost everything in my fire story would have blessed you!

- If you work for a large company with an electronic bulletin board, post your item(s). A coworker may know of a family in need at a house of worship, school, or club.

The first client who told me she wanted to know the person who would receive her donation had an abundance of clothing. I happened to know a newly divorced woman who was pouring all of her income into her four children. She needed but couldn't afford new clothes. My client filled my car with wardrobe items for her! When her husband heard what she was doing, he asked how old the boys in the family were. The next thing I knew, he was adding to the donation so the boys could have some suits and slacks. Ask around, and you'll find the direct donation you'll feel comfortable with. There is no shortage of those who need clothing, furniture, or kitchen items.

"I bought that when I was (in college, at my first job, pregnant, living in New York), and I just can't part with it, even though I know I should."

At least one of two emotional issues is at play here. First is the belief that if you hold on to the item, somehow that time in your life will be present. It won't. I'm sorry to be the one to tell you, but the trophies you won in high school athletics need to stop accompanying you in life. Take a photograph of you with them now and make a shadow box that shows you the day you earned each trophy or in your room at age fifteen surrounded by them. Your version of the high school trophy might be the texts you studied in law or medical school. I've seen boxes of these books eat up a living room occupied by people near retirement. Let's face it, a stack of schoolbooks isn't terribly interesting to look at, is it? Your particular albatross will be unique, but in the end it's going to be equally outdated and unneeded.

Second, people may hold on to the past through stuff because the past was so painful, they weren't really present for it. If sight of an item triggers a particular memory, they fear that if the item goes, so will the memory. You would be better served to cull your possessions that hold such memories and take into the future those that continue to serve and not just remind you. The remainder can be photographed and made into a physical or digital album you can peruse at your leisure. Even if you live in Windsor Castle, you don't want your space crowded with stuff with no use except as a memory trigger. Where will future mementos and useful items be kept? I've had clients live in near-hoarding conditions because it breaks their hearts to add to the city landfill. Guess what? You're living in one when you do this. Get involved in your city's trash and recycling programs, and do some real good for the community.

What Was That Mantra Again?

Remember when I cautioned you that focusing on the whole of the task of rightsizing would be overwhelming? Right about now you may be feeling cowed by the emotional work in front of you. You might be tempted to say, "Screw it! I'm taking it all, and I'll sort it at the other end." Or perhaps you feel that a series of pods or a storage unit are the answer. Pods are large portable storage units that are delivered to you by truck and parked in your driveway or on the street. (Do check local ordinances and with your apartment building management.) You load them at your leisure, and they are taken away when you are ready. They can be moved across town or across the country and stored indefinitely. This task will never be easy for you. You might as well face the music and do the sorting, purging, and decision making now. Besides, pods and storage units cost money, a lot of which you will waste if you delay the process for years, as several of my clients have done. They are wealthy, so the monthly check for these units doesn't impact them financially. The amount of money wasted, however, makes me cringe because it could be put to better use (a vacation, new clothing, a college fund for a child) or given to a charity. The latter would even yield a tax deduction, making it all the sweeter.

One Room at a Time

In this and the remaining chapters, I'm going to lay out the major rooms in any home. This week, we'll tackle the kitchen and laundry room. You might have to tailor the order in which you follow the guidelines to your personal situation. Feel free to work in the order that supports your speedy, organized exit.

I'm going to begin in the kitchen. It's the heart of any home and is usually one of the least organized. Why? Because on the day you moved in, your mother, sister, best friend, or coworker stopped by to assist you. The goal was to get out of boxes and the motto was, "You can organize everything later." The problem is that later almost never comes, and the turmoil in the cupboards and pantry simply feeds on itself.

Let's clear out the debris and make a plan for the new space. When I moved in late 2013, I was downsizing from twelve hundred to seven hundred square feet, and not wanting to find myself in a sea of possessions and no place to put them, I planned in advance where every single item was going to live. Toss what you can. If you can pack some items, that will make life easier for the movers. You can tell them, "The boxes in this room contain kitchen items, and that's the room they are going to in the new home." Get a black marker and write the destination on the box. If it gets separated from its brethren on the truck, there will be no confusion about

Creating uniform labels for your boxes is a snap if you have a computer. A Sharpie with a thick nib will also work wonders. For those of you who enjoy preprinted labels, check out the Tag-a-Room labeling system.

Remember, labels should be consistent and easy to understand. Consider creating coordinating room signs now for the new location so your movers know exactly where everything should go on moving day.

where it goes on arrival. Alternatively you can create labels on your computer, as they will be the easiest to read. A label maker won't really help you here because the print is too small. Some clients use color-coded labels or tape. I've used colored dots. A magic marker is as creative as you need to get! Be mindful when you are labeling boxes from one room that will go to a completely different room in the next location.

If you're just moving across town, I wouldn't bother with making an inventory. The mover will generate one, and you can check off the boxes at the other end. If I'm using a mover I trust and we only drove about eight miles, I don't even bother to do that because I know we left an empty house and drove straight to the new location. There's no chance for a box to vanish—unless, of course, you are in a big city and the truck will be open on the street for several hours. In that case, I enlist the help of a friend to sit on a chair by the truck with a good book and a bottle of water to make sure no one helps himself to a box. In some cities this would be unheard of; in others the truck would be stripped bare in seconds.

If you're moving a longer distance, and your boxes are going to be loaded at your current address, unloaded at a warehouse, and then reloaded onto a second truck for delivery, you would do well to have your own inventory. With the proliferation of smart phones and Excel, you can easily log the boxes. I would number them using preprinted numbers from an office-supply store. Be sure you identify the contents of your box on more than one side but always in the same spots. I frequently lose time when I unpack a client and have to hunt for a box's content identification. And finally, while it's OK to purchase boxes that have been used in a previous move, you need to cross out or cover the previous user's notations. You don't want your mover or professional organizer to have several boxes in the guest room that really belong in the kitchen. I remember unpacking a huge kitchen years ago, and it was a challenge to get everything to fit. About an hour after I'd finished the room, one of the mover's said to me, "Regina, I just found two more dish packs for the kitchen." I had to completely reorganize the room.

Clearing the Clutter: Packing the Kitchen

This week, we'll begin our rightsizing process with the kitchen and the laundry room. I've provided a list of questions to get you going in the kitchen and making decisions about which items to keep and which to eliminate.

Move systematically from one counter space to the next and from one upper cupboard to the next; then do the lower cabinets. Don't peer in and say, "Oh! I know I want everything here." Handle each item and give it due consideration. If you are on the fence, ask yourself what ties you to a given piece. When did you last use it? How likely are you to start using it again in the new digs?

After the cabinets, move to the pantry—if you're lucky enough to have one. (If you have a butler's pantry, work it the same way and know how very envious I am.) You might also want to include items in the dining room that spill over from the kitchen. I'm thinking of seldom-used dishes or table linens stored in a hutch, china cabinet, or sideboard. Very often a closet in this room secretly houses an extra set of dishes or a big space taker like a turkey roaster. This week it's all about cooking and entertaining decisions and the reality of these items being used in your new location. If you have always hosted Thanksgiving dinner but would like to pass the torch to another family member, ask if he or she wants the turkey roaster, deep fryer, and other accoutrements. If that person passes, donate them before you leave. Make someone else's Thanksgiving holiday special.

By the way, if you do decide to keep those rarely used dishes, why not store them in padded containers designed for this purpose? You can put these containers on your shopping list for the new house. If you have a china set, you or your movers will want to wrap each plate individually, so there's no point boxing the set up for storage right now. In the new home, however, padded containers will protect every item in the set.

Kitchen Questions

- Has any food expired? Remember to check any frozen foods. When freezing, make it a habit to mark down not only contents but also the date frozen. No more mystery meats!

- Spices are a touchy subject for most people. Even though a date indicates a product is long past its potency, you feel the need to hold on because the jar is so big and you don't want to be wasteful. It may be wiser in the future to purchase the smallest size of a spice and store it away from the heat of the stove and sunlight. In your next location, depending on the size of your kitchen or backyard, you may want to grow your basic herbs. In the meantime be realistic about what you should keep now.

- Is there any broken equipment you've been meaning to have fixed? Most people have kept that good intention alive for years.

Donate any such item to a charity like Goodwill so it can be fixed and sold—especially if you long ago replaced it.

- If you want to replace some items (when I moved I gave away my ancient blender and food processor and got new ones), start a list of those to be repurchased after you get to the new location. I use Amazon Prime for items I know I want and don't need to examine in person in a store. You may have another, similar outlet you prefer to use.

- Do you have multiples of items? Most of my clients have several garlic presses, wine openers, and potato peelers. This happens when households are merged or you hang on to grandmother's potato peeler as if it belongs in the Smithsonian. As I've said in other books, if grandma were alive, she'd be at Williams Sonoma buying a new one.

- Could you give multiple sets of dishes and glasses to family members?

- Have you outgrown some items? Can you toss your now teen-age children's sippy cups? Yes, I know, they may have children one day, and when they do, they will bring sippy cups when they come to visit you—new ones emblazoned with the super-heroes of the day.

- Have you hung onto items you have long since lost interest in? Maybe you were once a star baker or the queen of the slow cooker. It's probably cheaper to repurchase these items if your interest is rekindled than it is to pay movers to haul them to the new location.

- Does chipped china share space in the cupboard with what you call the good china? Are chipped glasses stashed away as if they would make a desirable set with the chipped china? Now is a great time to off-load those items. At IKEA, for about $20, you can get a set of dishes for four. Let's not set a table that looks like it's right out of *The Grapes of Wrath*.

- Will your linens work in the new space, or is it time to replace tablecloths, napkins, and placemats? Are they threadbare, stained, tattered, or torn? Give them a polite burial. And while you're at it, what about the window coverings? Will your kitchen curtains be useful in the new home or just an eyesore?

- If you own your refrigerator and stove, is it time to replace them? Are there newer versions at the next location? These are heavy items, so you want to arrange for their pickup on the day of your move so you don't have to get rid of them in the next city. Remember that the cost of your long-distance move is calculated by weight; paying to haul what you will ultimately donate will negate any tax deduction you might receive.

Planning for the Next Kitchen

We all have items that move with us from kitchen to kitchen, like that set of expensive cookware or our favorite china. Your new kitchen may be bigger, allowing you to spread your treasured items out and perhaps buy a few things you have long desired but had no counter space for, like a KitchenAid mixer. Promise me you won't schlep items you no longer need simply because you have a big kitchen with a lot of cupboards.

But what if the kitchen is smaller? Have you counted the cupboards and drawers? Are they deeper, narrower, or fewer in number? Do you have a place for everything you are packing? Take the time to solve these riddles now rather than be peppered with questions by Aunt Tilly on move-in day about where things go. If you say you don't know, she will shove everything into the cupboards, and later you will be asking, "Why didn't I make a plan when we were still in the old house?" Let's consider a few solutions to the most common problems.

- If the cupboards are too narrow for dinner plates (yes, this can happen if the designer sacrificed space for a Viking range or a picture window), you may want to use countertop plate stands. Small items like saucers, teacups, and salad plates can live in a cupboard.

- If you have a dining room china cabinet or hutch, divest it of items not related to entertaining, and use it for overflow items from your small kitchen. If the kitchen is normal size, however, do dedicate this piece of furniture to entertaining paraphernalia.

- Maximize cupboard space with an expandable shelf organizer, which instantly give you three levels rather than just the floor of the shelf. They come in three widths, so you can use one for vegetable or soup cans, another for spices, and perhaps a third for cans of dog or cat food.

- Items can get lost in deep cupboards. Where is that juicer? Oh yeah, it landed in the black hole of Calcutta (aka your deep cupboard). Install simple units that slide in and out so the back of any cabinet is always accessible.

- Store pot lids on the back of a cupboard door in a holder designed for that purpose or get a lid rack. You need cabinet space for the latter.

- Use shelf dividers in the pantry so that categories of food stay together.

- Use Grid Totes to keep your pastas corralled and your seasoning packets in one place. Imagine never wasting time searching for food items.

- I'm not a huge fan of lazy Susans, but some folks love them, and they can make small items more accessible. It's easier to spin your way to an item than it is to shove a bunch of bottles and jars aside to reach what you need.

- If you have little counter space, put up a magnetic board and store your knife collection there.

- A pot rack over the stove will save additional cupboard space. You can also put up a magnetic bar and hang pots using S-hooks.

If you put up magnetic strips, you can hang your knives. Both choices relieve crowded counters and cupboards.

- If you have a garage, invest in some large rubber totes and keep items you use seldom, like the turkey roaster or deep fryer, there.

- If you haven't already considered switching to nontoxic, green alternatives when it comes to cleaning and doing laundry, now is the perfect opportunity. Soap Nuts are a natural laundry detergent harvested in India and Nepal. When they are spent, you can add them to your compost. Several online stores carry them, including Amazon. Your best friends when it comes to cleaning naturally are lemons, baking soda, and white vinegar.

Packing the Laundry Room

This room is most often right off the kitchen, although sometimes I find it located near the bedrooms. If yours is situated in the latter location, feel free to read these instructions and do this elimination work when you get to the bedroom. Otherwise, this week you will take a look at all those laundry supplies. Here are some tips:

- Most people have multiple bottles of the same detergent or stain lifter open at one time. Consolidate your stash and recycle any empty containers.

- This room is very often the repository of single socks, items to be mended, and other wishful-thinking detritus. Let this be the day you step out on faith, knowing that it's OK to toss these orphan items.

- Are any freestanding cabinets or shelves in this room going with you? Be sure to tell the mover, and be certain you know where they are going in the next home. If they are to remain, do you have storage in the new home for the cleaning and laundry products that now reside near the washer and dryer? Make a plan to replace whatever you are leaving behind. Will you install shelves or purchase a new cupboard? With any luck, cupboards and shelves will already be in place.

- Will the washer and dryer be staying? If so, be sure you leave the warranty and instruction manual nearby, and do the same for any large kitchen equipment remaining on-site, like the oven, refrigerator, or outdoor grill.

Some people have a sense of space and can tell by looking what will fit in a designated area. I would be safe rather than sorry and take measurements for as many areas as you can before you move. You don't want to find out on the big day that the washer and dryer don't fit and you need to get a stackable unit. You also don't want to assume that you have the correct hookup in place. Be certain you are going from electric or gas to the same situation.

You also don't want to discover on moving day that the new place isn't clean. Be sure the landlord or previous owner is having someone come in to tidy up after the former occupants. I also would send over a second person of my choosing to disinfect the kitchen and bathrooms. If you like to use contact paper in kitchen drawers and shelves, this time-consuming task should be done in advance if possible. You don't want to be stalled on moving day because you have to measure and cut contact paper! A thick drawer liner is much easier to handle, and it's washable. You'll find it in big rolls at Bed Bath & Beyond.

If you are purchasing organizing tools in advance, see if you can drop them off at the new address or have them delivered and stored safely there. If you are moving to a rental, this is unlikely, but if you have purchased a home, escrow is sure to close a few days before the move, giving you some wiggle room.

Packing Tips for the Kitchen and Laundry

When it comes to breakables, don't be stingy with paper. Crumple lots of it on the bottom of the box (several inches worth), wrap each item like a newborn, and be sure that items can't shift in the box. Ideally no box is going to slip and fall onto pavement, but should that happen, you want to hear silence not shattering. One easy way to test your packing acumen is to shake what you consider a completed box. If you hear rattling, you need to add additional cushioning. If you hear silence you can pat yourself on the back for a job well done.

Boxes called "dish packs" are designed to handle dishes and glasses. Guard against making your boxes too heavy. Gauge the maximum weight by the strength of the folks doing the heavy lifting. The typical mover is a big guy in good shape. He can hoist a fifty-pound box with ease. If your family is top-heavy with women, you may want to restrict the boxes to thirty-five or forty pounds. And don't forget to rent a dolly. You'll want to stack boxes and move several at a time. Even if you have a huge crew, carrying boxes one by one will take forever. Trust me. I've seen it all.

Put the heaviest items on the bottom. You don't want your cookbooks sitting on top of your fine china. Actually, keep all categories of books in small boxes. Line them up so that the spines are facing upward, and stuff them in so that they can't move around. Paper of any kind (aside from packing paper, of course) makes for the heaviest boxes and I've seen grown men struggle when a client used a gigantic box for books, thinking it would be clever to pack a whole category in one big box. Movers have insurance, but like the rest of us, they appreciate it when you help them avoid a hernia.

The most common mistake I see is dishes packed in stacks. If the box drops, the stack breaks like it received a karate chop. Wrap each plate individually and place them vertically, nested into each other. If you have a special set of dishes stored in padded holders, I'd take them out and wrap them individually. To the best of your ability, keep all parts of a set or pieces of an item in the same box. When my movers packed me, they were just in from a job on the road and exhausted. I presume this is why they packed my kitchen like a giant puzzle. I'd find a pot in one box and the lid several boxes later. They even packed my fine china flat after we had discussed the importance of standing dishes up. Exhaustion has a funny way of overriding your common sense, no matter how experienced you are.

Remember to pad between the heaviest, medium-weight, and lightest items in a box. You can pack your sheets, towels, and all linens in a separate box, or you can use them as cushioning. This saves on paper, but remember you'll have a lot of laundry at the other end. If you have a laundry room or a washer-dryer combo, you can do this as you unpack. Trekking to a separate laundry room in an apartment building, however, will add to your workload. When you make choices over the next few weeks, think them all the way through.

To repeat: I'm a firm believer in having the pros pack my breakables. They will do it better and faster than I can. (My mover didn't use the correct technique, but he used so much packing paper that the dishes arrived unscathed.) Remember, you don't necessarily have to begin packing now if you've hired someone to pack for you or doing so would be too disruptive—but you should definitely tackle the elimination portion of the program this week and pack when it is best for you.

When you do start boxing up, pack in advance items that you won't need and that can't break, like canned goods, cookbooks, and linens. You may even want to pack some of your pots and pans or appliances like your mixer or food processor. I doubt you have any gourmet meals planned for before the move. If you are going to pack the dishes and glassware, decide how many to leave out for everyday use. Some families resort to paper products before a move. That's a personal choice—I'd suggest you save a tree and just wash the dishes. But choose what works for you, and for heaven's sake don't embrace guilt.

If you are lucky enough to have the funds to pay your movers to do all of the packing, then this week will be about elimination only. Food-storage containers missing lids and or lids missing bottoms should go into the recycle bin. Toss the wicker basket of socks without mates. This is the week to get lean and mean in the kitchen and laundry area. This is also the ideal week to shed any leftover belongings from previous relationships. I had a client whose husband stashed his ex's cooking equipment and dishes on high shelves in their kitchen. Unless you plan to invite an ex over to cook, it's time to make a donation. But if that includes a $1,200 coffeemaker that you use religiously every morning, then what can I say? Take it with you. There's an exception to every rule, isn't there?

Finally, don't attempt to label a box with every single item it contains. As you get tired, those details will drive you insane. Try listing categories instead. Any method you choose is fine, but be sure you communicate your labeling style to every family member or friend who is helping. Nothing is more confusing than unpacking boxes packed by a group of people with their own ideas about labeling. And once again, if you are reusing boxes (I purchased recycled boxes from my mover), make sure only your labels are showing. You don't want to wonder whether a box has living room or bedroom items because you don't recognize the handwriting of the friend who packed it. The devil is truly in this kind of detail on moving day.

You can learn how to pack specific items or use a dolly, among other moving day skills, online. I'd try YouTube.com, eHow.com, About.com, and MyMove.com. The last will send you all sorts of useful information. After I signed up for my move, the site offered tips about my city and triggered discount coupons from major retailers.

Kitchen Moving-Day Box

Think ahead to moving day. Make a list of the items you'll need in an emergency kitchen box. Be sure you mark it "load last" so it will be first off the truck. You'll have a few of these boxes, so be sure to set them to one side and explain to the movers how important they are to you. You can attach wild stickers to all "load last" boxes for easy visual identification.

My moving-day kitchen box would have my coffeemaker, coffee, toaster, and some food I might prepare quickly, like instant oatmeal, a few bags of raw nuts, a loaf of bread, and paper plates, cups, and cutlery. Your box will be unique to you, your family, and the number of people assisting you. I'd be sure to have an ample supply of bottled water for everyone involved. You can always pack a cooler if you have a large one. If you're taking it anyway, it might as well serve a function.

Some people store medicine and first aid supplies in the kitchen. You can pop in a few basics (the operative words are "few" and "basic"). Be sure you have prescription medications readily available. Whether you make a different box or pack these with the kitchen items, they must be easy to find on the big day. And please don't forget that Fido and Fifi will need to have breakfast and dinner. Pack meals for them, as well as their bowls and meds. They may need to be quarantined in a bathroom at the new address, and you don't want to have to scramble for a water bowl, treats, and most especially medication. In most big cities now, chain stores like Petco and Pet Smart provide doggie day care. This is another alternative to preserve your furry family members from the turmoil of the big day. Make your reservation well in advance as you will have to register your furry friends as first-time guests. These chains need to be sure your pet has no fleas and is up-to-date on shots, and so forth. Check out their websites for specifics.

This is a key box, so start thinking about its contents and make a list you can add to over the next several weeks. If you are driving behind the truck, you can pop your box or cooler into the trunk of your car. If your new residence is a long way away and you're driving behind the moving van, you will have to give more thought to this box. Are you staying in hotels and eating out or munching in the room? You get the idea. Tailor your box to your needs. And if you have small children, be sure to have ample snack food handy, no matter the distance to your new home. A friend who can't help on moving day might be able to assemble your kitchen box the night before, provided you can supply a list of items needed. I have found that friends and family prefer following specific steps. And that allows you to let helpers tackle the tasks they are good at. Give each assignment some consideration. Remember, this is your move, and you have a right to call the shots. The person who whines, "Please let me do it my way. I'm just trying to help you," should stay home.

Kitchen Exit Ritual

In *The 8-Minute Organizer*, most chapters end with "exit rituals," a set of tasks to perform each time you leave a room. I decided to include the one for the kitchen here so that you have a better chance of keeping order in your next residence.

Here's the exit ritual for the heart of the home:

- Put away all food.
- Wash dirty dishes or put them in the dishwasher.
- Put away clean dishes.
- Wash any pots and pans, except those that need to soak for a while.
- Return kitchen tools to their designated spots.
- Give the table and counters a quick wipe.
- Check the trash for food items, such as banana peels, that will become aromatic over the next few hours. Consider purchasing a stainless steel or ceramic compost pail for wet garbage.
- Turn off the overhead light.

You can create an exit ritual for every room. You'll find the steps become second nature after a short time. Assign a room to a child and have him check it before bed or first thing in the morning. It's a great chore.

Week's Summary

- ❑ Meet with representatives from at least three moving companies. If you decide to hire one, book your move this week.
- ❑ If you are planning a self-move, get prices for the tools you need to rent, like a truck and a dolly. Be sure they are available on the day you will need them.
- ❑ Secure transport for unusual, valuable, or outsized items like artwork or a piano.
- ❑ If you are shipping your vehicle, investigate your options.
- ❑ If your household is moving many miles and you are shipping your vehicle, research plane, train, or bus tickets.

❑ Engage friends and family for specific move-related duties. If you are doing a self-move, you need a mix of strong and organized friends.

❑ Be sure the charity of your choice will accept the items you wish to donate and can pick them up on the day you designate.

❑ Begin dealing with the emotional issues that threaten to keep you attached to items you no longer need, want, or use or that you can't fit into the new space.

❑ Clean out cupboards and drawers in the kitchen.

❑ Pack some items if time permits and you have decided not to let the pros simply do it all.

❑ Begin making a shopping list of helpful items you'll need in your next kitchen.

❑ Start planning a kitchen moving-day box to be loaded onto the truck last.

A Closing Thought

This is a very busy and emotional week for those of you who have big items to donate and kitchen items to evaluate. The rubber hits the road this week as you realize just how much work lies ahead of you. If you focus on that, you will make yourself even more exhausted. Remember that each decision represents one more issue you don't have to revisit and one less item on your to-do list. You are closer to that fresh start than you were last week. As items get picked up, donated, and given away, the energy in your home will shift dramatically. This week the reward should involve getting out of the house. How about having dinner at your favorite neighborhood spot, taking in a movie, or asking a dear friend to watch the kids so you and your partner can have a few quiet hours together? You deserve it.

TELL THE WORLD AND TAKE ANOTHER STEP

There are two mistakes one can make
along the road to truth . . .
. . . not going all the way, and not starting.
—BUDDHA

WEEK THREE CAN BE PIVOTAL BECAUSE, ONCE AGAIN, THE SIZE of the project may feel overwhelming and tempt you to procrastinate. You need to dig deep, keep up all the self-care actions that appeal to you, and think ahead to moving day. You want to envision a smooth move that leaves you with the task of unpacking but filled with joy that a new chapter in your life has officially started. The more detailed this vision is, the more likely you will be to make it happen. Call this opening my sneaky way of suggesting yet another tool for your self-care arsenal: creative visualization. It's so easy to get into "negative speak" right about now and to start expecting the worst.

SELF-CARE TIP FOR THE WEEK

IF THE PHRASE "creative visualization" gives you New Age aches and pains, look at it this way. We live in a cause-and-effect universe, right? Every action has a reaction. If you pack your possessions in nice categories and off-load the excess as you go, it's going to be easier to find a new home for everything at the other end. If you postpone key elements of this move until the last minute, you will no doubt have a moving nightmare. One logically follows the other. My mother saw the glass as half empty and expected the worst at every turn. Perhaps saying, "I knew this was going to happen!" whenever disaster struck made her feel more powerful. I rarely knew my mother to be happy. I'd like you to avoid her self-created misery. It's just an idea.

Be conscious and fight those impulses when they arise. Who knows, this move might just make you an avowed optimist.

This week you will start thinking about all the people who need to know you are moving, from Aunty Tilly to your dentist. And you will attack the master bedroom. In many homes the common rooms are tidy, while the bedroom is chaotic. At week's end you'll be able to say you've vanquished one of the toughest areas in the home. And just so you have an increasing sense of reality about this move, we're going to pack a box or two. You can't deny you're on your way out the door once you see some packed boxes!

Mail Call: Prepare Your Forwarding Paperwork

I want to give you a little mental work in week three to prepare for the weeks ahead. After all, you need to husband your physical strength as we march toward moving day, especially if you have young children, are a single parent, or work full-time. There is no question that each of these situations adds stress because you are probably already running on near empty when it comes to physical stamina and emotional reserves. Let's try to make life a wee bit easier, shall we?

This week, prepare to have mail forwarded to your new address. If you live in the United States, the postal service allows you to file a change-of-address form online. If you aren't computer literate, stop by your local post office and pick up the form this week. I would file it two weeks before your truck arrives. Make a note on your calendar to file the paperwork in week six so this doesn't fall through the cracks. I would also let your mail carrier know that you plan to leave. The couple that lived in my current apartment had a snafu with the post office, and for weeks I had their mail in my box. On the other hand, the day after I moved in, I received my first piece of mail. Clearly you have to make an offering to the mail gods, which is why I suggest you let your carrier and your local post office know, in addition to submitting the online change-of-address form. This may seem like overkill, but missing a check, a 1099, or a communication from a legal entity is an unnecessary frustration.

Certain items can be left to chance, like junk mail and donation requests from charities. Trust me, they will eventually find you. But your bills are another matter. If you have access to a computer, it's easiest to let every financial institution know via its official company website. If you are a pen-and-paper person, create a template letter and then tweak it for each entity. If you are a phone person, schedule a block of time to make calls. For now, make a list of the institutions, service providers, and individuals you need to contact, such as the following:

- Accountant
- Agent(s) (if you are in the arts)

- Attorney(s)
- Bank(s) (order checks with your new address)
- Cable provider
- Credit card(s)
- DMV
- Doctors, hospitals, and dentist
- Family and friends
- Insurance agent(s)
- IRS
- Magazines and newspapers to which you have subscriptions
- Social Security Office
- Telephone provider(s) (land line and cell)
- Union(s)
- Utilities
- Veterinarian if you have pets
- Voter registration office

Your list may include items omitted here. Making a list allows you to avoid flying by the seat of your pants and wondering later whom you did and did not contact. Set aside some time this week to contact every person and entity listed, and set up a file for address-change confirmations. This is a big task best accomplished in a timely fashion. Of course, the caveat is that you need to know your new address, and you may still be searching for the new location. If you prefer to wait, be sure this gets done at least two weeks before the big day and that you schedule the task on your calendar. As the weeks roll by, you are going to be more and more physically and mentally exhausted and overwhelmed. No important task can be left to chance! This may be the perfect time to switch all of your bill paying to an online or automatic format so you never have to worry about a bill not finding its way to you. A missed payment can automatically ding your FICO score.

If your new residence is in the same town, you will find many of these notifications easy because you are stopping and starting service with the same company. The task is a bit more complicated when you have to move to a new city and find out if your bank has a branch there and who will supply your electric, gas, and other household services. Dealing with corporations makes me want to weep. You get transferred from one department to another and find yourself at the mercy of the system in place and the intelligence and even the mood of the person at the other end. I would definitely schedule a block of time to knock out as many of these calls in one sitting as is possible. And I would fortify myself with a good meal and a few gallons of water. It's bound to be a bumpy ride. A little trick is to remember the name of the representative who answers and to use it. And have compassion for someone who is probably abused verbally several times a day by irate customers. Kindness will smooth your journey.

Are you moving to a new city? Ask your current health providers if they have any recommendations. (Be sure your current health-care plan covers any providers recommended. If you don't have insurance at the moment, don't be shy about negotiating a cash price for a doctor's services.) Give your current providers a heads-up that your new doctors will be calling them to transfer records. As we move ever more fully into the digital age, these transfers are becoming a snap. We tend to forget that we have a legal right to our medical records. Some offices charge a fee for the transfer but none can refuse you. When you get to your new city, locate the nearest hospital or urgent-care center, especially if you have children.

To Be or Not to Be a Geek

That is the question. When it comes to using technology during your move, always do what is right and comfortable for you. I have a famous and wealthy friend who wouldn't own a smart phone if her life depended on it. I have a financially comfortable relative who wants no part of any technology. I have friends who tell me I must have a digital calendar and a Gmail address, or I'll be labeled old-fashioned. I am reminded of a wonderful phrase I wish I had coined: "the tyranny of the shoulds."

Even if you like a particular app or computer program, you have to input the data and actually use the program to be successful, right? I guarantee you'll be working the Magic Formula whether you're holding a mouse, stylus, or pencil. That's why I'm giving you options, for instance when it comes to mail forwarding. Make calls. Go online. Write letters. Some options may be faster than others, but only the end result matters. I can fly to New York from Los Angeles, take a train or a bus, or drive. As long as I get there, the means of travel is irrelevant. As you read, I think Excel will be the easiest place to make lists if you don't want to use an app, but if a yellow legal pad floats your boat, then that's what you should use.

Organization apps and websites are constantly appearing in the marketplace, and existing ones like Google Calendar, Cozi, and Evernote are the standard bearers. They are all wonderful for different reasons. The idea is to use an easy and intuitive form of technology that makes information about your move accessible to your family and friends. Here are a few more incredibly helpful, albeit specialized, apps brought to you from my favorite technology website, Techlicious.com. They will keep you on an organized track long after you have unpacked the last box.

- AboutOne: This app is great for the intact family at any time, not just during a move. You can share a calendar and store key items, like medical information, a home inventory, and photos and videos.
- Two Happy Homes: This app is great for divorced parents trying to coordinate their households. Parents can keep a joint calendar and contact list and even track and pay expenses.
- CareZone: This app helps people care for loved ones. You can keep a journal updating everyone involved; store important documents that a caregiver might need at any time; and track medications, dosages, prescriptions, and even doctor's visits.
- Pet Master Pro: This app is for those with furry children who need to track medications, vaccination records, microchip information, and even vet, groomer, or day care appointments.

If you're moving out of the area, Fido and Fifi will need a recommendation for a new vet (perhaps someone who went to school with or knows your current one), the location of the nearest emergency animal hospital, specific animal control regulations for new pet residents, and the deadlines for filing the necessary papers. If you have a smart phone, download the Red Cross's free Pet First Aid app. It can save a furry life in an emergency. And be sure your pets are microchipped.

Upending the Inner Sanctum: Packing the Master Bedroom

This week, we're going to examine the master bedroom—perhaps the most important room in the home. I frequently go into homes and find a pristine environment in the living areas. I wonder why this person or couple feels the need for a professional organizer. And then I enter the master bedroom, and it's like seeing the soul of the house. This is where chaos most commonly resides and hides. Tackling the master suite is such a complicated prospect for most that I'm going to give you two weeks to get it ready. Next week I'll provide instructions for the master bathroom. Once you have the entire master suite under control, all ancillary bedrooms and bathrooms will follow suit using the same basic instructions. We'll work on kids' bedrooms during week seven (pages 181–198).

For now, let's begin with a few master bedroom questions. A move is a great time to get real about clothing, an emotionally charged subject for many people, so grab some water and a few healthy snacks, and meet me in the bedroom.

Bedroom Questions

- Are you taking all of your bedroom linens with you? Will the colors work in the new location? Has your supply grown old, threadbare, tattered, or faded while you weren't looking? Purchase new linens after you move so you don't have to pack them. And donate your discards to an animal hospital or shelter. They always need bed linens and old towels. You won't get a tax deduction, but you will get some great karma.

- Will the bedspread or duvet and window treatments work in the new location, or do they need to be replaced?

- If you plan to use the same mattress and box spring in your new home, be sure you get covers for them. The covers can be laundered after the move. You can ask your movers to provide covers, but I think they are a good idea in general, so I would invest now if you haven't already.

- If it's time to replace your mattress, have the new one ordered and waiting at the new location.

- The linen closet is usually near the master bedroom, so take a look at your entire supply of sheets, towels, duvets, blankets, and so forth. Remember that the puppies and kitties at shelters and animal hospitals need these items, so take only what you really use and donate the rest.

- Do you have "fat" clothes from another time in your life? Why are you keeping them? Do you plan to gain weight in the new location? I didn't think so. Make a donation bag or box. (Use heavy-duty black or green trash bags, not the flimsy white ones).

- Do you have a stash of "skinny" clothes from the time before you had children? Was that several years ago? I support you in your quest to lose weight, but unless it's an active goal, let's let these items go to a charity. When you lose the extra weight, you won't want to celebrate by wearing outdated items from years ago. A little celebrating in the form of shopping will be in order.

- Were you in corporate America a few years ago? Do you have suits and formal business wear from that period? Why not donate these to Dress for Success and help someone get started in a new career? If you return to corporate America, you will need to dress in current styles. Dress for Success accepts business wear from men and women. And yes, it is a tax deduction.

- If you are moving from a cold climate to a more moderate one, you probably won't need a huge stash of winter coats. New York Cares has a coat drive each year. See if the city you are leaving has a similar program and help the less fortunate stay warm.

- If moving to a moderate climate, you may not need snow or rain boots or other inclement-weather items, like hats, gloves, and heavy sweaters. When I moved from New York to Los Angeles, I couldn't fathom never needing these items again. How could it be mild all year long? Over time I divested myself of my heavy outer wear, retaining one pair of snow boots and one heavy coat for those periodic winter trips home.

- If, on the other hand, you are moving to a colder climate and you will be arriving in winter, you will want basic cold-weather wear. But get only the basics because you'll score better deals and find a wider selection in cities where these garments are needed and worn. Heavy woolens, for example, aren't sold in Los Angeles. When would we wear them?

- Were you once an avid skier, and do you have a wardrobe just for that activity? Any sport comes with accoutrements, and a move is a good time to ask if you are done with them. If you ever decide to pick the sport back up, you can check out Craigslist. org and score some deals. In the meantime another avid skier can use the stuff that's now nothing more than a space-hogging homage to the past.

- Do you have clothing that you think of as a potential costume? Unless your family goes all-out each Halloween, please donate these items to a charity or perhaps to the local community the- ater. I've organized women in their forties and fifties who still have their cheerleading outfits. Find a photograph of you in your outfit and frame it in a shadow box with a swatch of the outfit's fabric. Or put that swatch in an album next to a photo of you doing a Herkie. Even if you weigh the same as you did in high school, there comes a time when you just can't pull off that costume.

- You now have an opportunity to go fearlessly through your shoe collection and see which from your past will continue to serve you in the future. Be realistic. I once worked with a famous ac- tress with an impressive collection of Manolo Blahniks. We put them in acrylic shoe drawers so she could see her collection at a glance. And she generously gave almost forty pairs to a women's shelter. If she could part with her Manolos, you can part with the shoes you know in your heart you aren't going to wear again.

- Don't forget to go through your dresser drawers and do anoth- er fearless inventory. Perhaps this move is the impetus you need to toss out threadbare underwear, old pajamas, and socks with no partners.

- I like to keep the area under the bed clear, but many people store items there in makeshift containers or drawers. Do go through these.
- If you have the dimensions of your new bedroom, will your current furnishings fit in the new space? Will you have to eliminate a dresser or nightstand? Can they be repurposed in the new home? Or is your new bedroom larger, and can you now shop for a comfy reading chair?
- If items are to be given away or donated, make appointments now to have them picked up the week before the move. If your charity or friends bail on you, you'll still have time to find another source. Add these calls to the ones you are making for your address changes.

Packing Tips for Clothing and Linens

Clothing is easy to pack because it can't break. You don't have to be a professional mover to put soft items in a box, then seal and label it. You do have to decide what you can live without for the next few

I knew a divorced man who saw his young son periodically because they lived on opposite coasts. He had a robust supply of white T-shirts, undershirts, and those wonderful items called "wife beaters" that would rival the current stock at any Macys. When I asked if we could perhaps cull the collection, he told me he was saving them for his son. "Really?" I thought. "Your son is going to want your old shirts when he's a young man? Why? Because they have designer labels?" As we used to say in Brooklyn, "Get a real idea." Dad had something of a hoarding issue with clothing and dressed it up in poetic terms. If you find yourself hanging on to clothing you do not wear, ask yourself if you have real reasons to keep it.

weeks. The obvious choice is off-season clothing. In the middle of winter, I don't need ready access to my bathing suit. If you are a very social person, you may need to keep out a special outfit for a scheduled night on the town; otherwise, you can pack up your party clothes.

Hanging clothing can stay as is because you'll be putting them into a special "wardrobe box." If you're using a professional mover, be sure you ask that these be put on the truck last so that they will be first off. If you organize your hanging clothes before packing them, you can just lift them out of the box and place them into the new closet. You want out of these boxes quickly so you don't have to pay for them. Some companies will charge you a small rental fee, but many will allow you to use the boxes gratis if you pack them the day of the move and return them as the movers exit your new home for the last time. If you damage the boxes or need to hold on to them for a few days or weeks, expect to incur a fee. If you are moving yourself, you will have to purchase these boxes, but you can easily resell them on Craigslist or perhaps a bulletin board at work. You can post your intention well in advance and have your buyer in place. These may be the most useful and coveted boxes around.

Wardrobe boxes are tall, so you can put shoes and boots at the bottom. There's little likelihood your clothes and footwear will make contact, as the boxes are rarely dropped and seldom tip over. Check out The Container Store's acrylic shoe drawers. Have a stash waiting at the new location. You can keep your best shoes visible, clean, and stored safely. If you purchase these shoe drawers in advance of the move, don't place them full in the bottom of the wardrobe boxes. They are too fragile for the rough-and-tumble they will encounter. Be sure you securely wrap the filled containers with paper before you place them in large flat boxes with lots of protective paper padding on the bottom.

Now is a great time to divest yourself of those evil wire hangers and dry cleaner plastic bags. The former destroy your clothing over time, and the latter seal in potentially carcinogenic chemicals and take up space in your closet. I personally use wood hangers, but the new huggable hangers are thinner, kind to clothes, and treated so that no fabrics will fall onto the floor. Invest and change over now.

On the Internet I've seen the self-move trick of wrapping sections of hanging clothes in a garbage bag with tape sealing the bag around the hangers. I think it's going to be a miracle if the clothing isn't wrinkled at the other end; however, if you are doing a self-move and need to save money, this is certainly one economical way to go. Remember to use heavy-duty bags, not flimsy, white kitchen trash bags. There's no point wrapping clothing in a bag destined to tear. If you have a car and are moving piecemeal over the course of several days, you can lay your bags on the back seat. In a truck, I have no clue how you'd secure them. Although I've seen this solution, I don't recommend it.

If you want to leave clothing items in your dresser drawers, you can add moving paper to keep things in place. This will save you having to pack and unpack those items. You'll be good to go in the new space. Your mover will place the paper for you, but expect contents to have shifted. A little tidying up may be in order! Your mover will insist that the items be lightweight clothing. Don't sneak in collectibles or artwork and make those good people stop to pack everything unless of course you're paying them to pack the entire contents of the home. Time is always money, but it's especially so on moving day. If you do something that slows the process, you will be responsible for the extra time. I once had a client who wouldn't let the movers take some pieces of furniture up a flight of stairs to her bedroom. We had no clue why she refused. She actually insisted they use a pulley system to haul the furniture up one story and bring it in through the window. It was insane. It took extra time. And they went over the estimate as they assured her they would.

Closets in the Other Bedroom(s)

If you have a dedicated guest room, I bet you use some of the closet space for off-season clothing. As these closets function as an extension of the master closet, you'll want to go through them this week. In general, after you cull unneeded garments (if you wore them often, you wouldn't keep them here, hidden with the off-season pieces!), the remainder should be easy to pack. If nothing can be folded, you or the mover or a friend can easily whip the collection into a wardrobe box on moving day. Decide now where this group will live in the new home. Is another guest closet waiting, or will you have to integrate these items into the master closet? Wardrobe boxes are costly and take up a lot of space. You want to know exactly where

Using suitcases to pack and store clothes is a great way to save on boxes. Many of my clients store smaller suitcases inside bigger ones to save space. But I'd ask you to remember where those smaller bags have been on your travels. Most likely a restaurant floor or maybe even a bathroom stall with no hooks. Now you're going to put that bag inside a bigger one that will ultimately hold your clothing. Gag! Use your suitcases to save money, but don't store them inside each other to save room. If they are attractive and you are strapped for space, you can store off-season clothing in them in the new home. Set them out in the bedroom and plop a lamp on top. This works for vintage or perhaps a set of Louis Vuitton. Check out some images at Pinterest as that is where I discovered this clever idea.

all of your clothing is going on the big day so you don't get stuck with the boxes. (I know I've said this before, but because details like this are critical and easy to miss, I repeat them regularly.)

If the guest bedroom is also an office, we'll get to office items in week five. Clothing and paper carry a lot of emotion and usually guilt, so I don't want to wear you out on week three! Children's rooms will also have a week of their own. With that said, you want to encourage older children to be ready to make decisions with you on the day you designate or to give you permission to make decisions for them. If they are late teens, they should be able to pack their own boxes.

Never make decisions for other family members without permission unless they are under the age of five and not able to grasp the task and its consequences. We all feel violated when our stuff gets tossed or goes missing. Teaching your children decision-making and organizing skills will be an enormous gift. You want to enter the new home on a positive note. And here's a heads-up for new parents who often use their child's closet as an adjunct to their own. On moving day this may be one of your temporary solutions. Be aware, however, that children grow quickly, and they don't need or want your stuff hogging their space.

Bedroom Moving-Day Box

You want linens for the bed at the ready. Your bedroom won't be unpacked for a few days, but at least you can sleep on clean sheets with your favorite pillows and, depending on the season, adequate blankets. You might want to do one box for each bedroom, especially if your children are old enough to make up their own beds. The movers won't leave until your beds are set up and all the furniture is in place.

The wardrobe boxes will go on the truck last, so hanging garments won't be difficult to grab. (This is standard practice, but be sure you and your mover are on the same page about these boxes coming off first.) Pack fresh underwear and an outfit for the next day in a small suitcase or medium-size box. It's miserable to wonder where in the world fresh underwear is located. And Fido and Fifi will be miserable if they don't have their favorite toys and beds.

Planning for the Next Bedroom

The big question always has to do with the next closet situation. In the best of all worlds you'll have at least the same-size closet or perhaps a walk-in. I had one in my last apartment and it was heaven. I had additional shelves added to maximize the space. It's so common to have one shelf in a closet with a huge amount of wasted space above it. The existing low shelf can be for current clothing choices, like sweaters or purses, while the upper one can hold off-season clothing in pretty storage boxes.

Here are some additional ideas to consider as you plan the new space:

- If the space is bigger than what you have now, plot out how you will separate your wardrobe and where you will hang things. If you can switch out your hangers now and divide by type (e.g., for shirts, slacks, and suits) and color code your garments (keep all whites, blacks, reds, and so forth, in any category together), you can put your clothes in the wardrobe boxes ready to be removed and hung directly in their new spot on moving day.

- To hang or to fold is an age-old question. If your closet is smaller, you may need to fold more and perhaps invest in a second dresser. If the space is bigger, you might start hanging items like blue jeans. Whatever maximizes the space is the best choice for you.

- Armoires are great for adding more hanging space to a bedroom. If you don't wish to spend the money, you can find clothing racks with natural cotton hanging storage bags to protect your garments. These are a bit cumbersome for everyday use but may save needed space in your closet. You can use them for off-season storage or for rarely worn items, like formal wear, costumes, or business suits (for the person who telecommutes, for example).

- Do you need a canvas shoe bag to hang over the next closet door to hold your workout shoes and summer sandals?

- Will you need a shoe stand of some sort to place your everyday shoes on for ease of retrieval?

- Would you like some acrylic shoe drawers to store your dress shoes? You'll be able to keep them stacked on a high shelf in the new closet, saving floor space for your everyday choices. The boxes are a tad pricey, so you might just want a few for your evening shoes.

- If you live in a cold climate, you will no doubt have a large collection of sweaters. Are you happy with how you store them now? If not, you might try a few acrylic sweater drawers or some sweater bags. Do keep some cedar chips in with them to keep moths out.

- One of my clients called a rug merchant and discovered that ancient traders packed tobacco pouches in with their rugs to deter moths. You can make some using cheesecloth. Your clothing will not smell like cigarettes. Burning tobacco has an acrid smell; fresh tobacco from a can is quite lovely. Lavender sachets and cedar chips are additional choices.

- If you are moving to a space with a second closet, you can use that for off-season storage. If you are losing a guest room or office with a large closet, you can try space bags, under bed containers, or the hall closet.

- Are your dresser drawers chaotic? Would some bra, panty, boxer/brief, or sock containers help you maintain order? They come in a variety of styles and price points.

- If you are having a custom closet designed, be sure you ask for a "telescoping valet bar" so you can plan outfits or use it for dry cleaning (until you can put the clothes away). This is a metal bar that pulls out from a recessed area in the closet. You just push it back when you're done!

- Hooks can also be installed on a door or simply cupped over the top to give you several inches of hanging space. That's the poor man's version of the telescoping valet bar.

- If you are designing a closet with stacked hanging spaces, be sure your designer uses one of the garments you're going to hang on the high rod as a guide. I once unpacked a couple who'd had a custom closet built using a very expensive wood. To preserve its appearance they had only the necessary holes drilled. Unfortunately the husband was very tall, and his shirts dragged on the items hanging on the lower rod. The designer never checked. We had to have more holes drilled. We lost time waiting for the carpenter to arrive. It made moving day that much more expensive and chaotic.

- Very often a shelf is placed over the lower rod in a stacked hanging situation. It looks lovely, but what do you realistically put there? If you need shelves, have a lower rod and then a series of shelves above. Discuss all options with your closet designer.

Time Suckers: Behaviors to Avoid

Contrary to what you might hope, this section is not about a new lollypop put out by a watch manufacturer. It does refer to the multitude of ways we human beings waste time because we're exhausted, depressed, dehydrated, or simply suck at time management. We need to shore up some of the leaks in the system to generate energy for this move. I want you to read the following list and then watch your behavior this week to see how many ways you waste time. I guarantee you do. It's a human thing, and on a normal day it

If circumstances force you to move back home with your parents or into the home of a generous friend, you most likely won't be top-heavy with possessions. You have the best chance for a successful stay if you make it your business to fit seamlessly into the existing family pattern. Find out when the family goes to bed so your music won't disturb them. Ask when they use the computer or exercise equipment in the guest room. Learn about meal times and other family rituals. If you have dietary restrictions, don't burden your hosts. Take care of your own food needs. Now is not the time to announce how you like to live life. "Compromise" is the watchword when you're merging households, but "respect" governs guests of all stripes. You want the host to say, "Darn, I sure miss that guy!" as you exit for the last time rather than "I thought he'd never leave!"

may not matter, but for the next few weeks, there are no moments to fritter.

- You give yourself five minutes to check your e-mail. An hour later you can't imagine where the time went.

- You need to relax so you give yourself ten minutes for social media. Two hours later it's after midnight, and you have work to turn in the next day. Another sleep-deprived day looms.

- You go to the store without a list because you are certain you know what you need. Once there you are distracted by a dizzying array of items and waste time and money on unnecessary purchases.

- You feel guilty if you don't answer the phone. You give chitchat time away when you need to be focused on the move.

- You love to read and decide to give yourself fifteen minutes a day before the move. When you look at the clock, you are stupefied by how much time has passed.

- You start the day with a carefully crafted to-do list but fritter time away by helping others or tackling every single request that comes your way. No is not yet in your vocabulary. People who put themselves in this position very often want to be released from the tasks they have to accomplish, and the request is the perfect excuse.

You get the idea. Don't waste a second on guilt, shame, or self-recrimination. You do these things because you are a human being. I'm merely suggesting that for the next few weeks, you need to be conscious when temptation arises and stay on track. Your cell phone has a timer. If you can spare fifteen minutes on social media, make it fifteen and not a second longer. If your to-do list is long and unnecessary requests for help come your way, simply decline this opportunity to be of service. Others will follow in due course. You are the captain of this ship, not a prisoner traveling in steerage.

Week's Summary

- ☐ Make a list of people and entities that need to know your new address as well as all businesses that serve your home.
- ☐ Clear out the items from your bedroom that need not make the journey with you.
- ☐ Pack some items, as this will give you a sense of accomplishment. Pack items in this room that do not wrinkle easily. If nothing else get the off-season clothing in a box.
- ☐ Consider which organizing tools will help you enjoy your wardrobe more and preserve it.
- ☐ Check for the secret time suckers in your life.

A Closing Thought

You may feel especially tired this week because going through clothing is difficult even when it's the only task on the docket. When you place it in the middle of a whirlwind eight-week ramp-up to a move, it's really tough. We have to slog through bad choices, old memories, and probably multiple sizes. Nature is known to be healing; in fact, traditional Chinese medicine holds that time spent in nature is good for the liver. Do you live near a park, botanical garden, the ocean, or some other glorious piece of Mother Nature? Spend some quiet time there before the new week, with its assignments, rolls into view. If you can, take the dog with you. He has no clue what you're up to and really wishes you would stop robbing him of floor space with all these boxes. He needs some nature too.

RUB-A-DUB-DUB,
LOTS OF FOLKS IN THIS TUB

Mistakes are the portals of discovery.

—JAMES JOYCE

LET ME ASSURE YOU, THE ROAD TO MOVING WILL HAVE ITS share of bumps. I want you to do the best you can without questing for perfection. Hopefully, the things that go wrong will be so unimportant you'll find them funny. Some of them may be outside your control, so if the rainstorm of the decade hits the day the truck arrives don't reach for the Johnny Walker—turn on the Comedy Channel app instead. And if something you do to cut corners or save money or time backfires, just know that mistake won't plague your next move. I learned about moving from two sources: the clients I helped, and the mistakes I made in my youth. The bottom line is this: human beings craft and carry out a move, and the best of us are flawed.

SELF-CARE TIP
FOR THE WEEK

YOU MAY CURRENTLY use and enjoy this week's self-care tip. I want you to consider the value of music while you work. If you're alone in a house, you might even burst out singing and feel so much better about the whole process. Dance around as you pack a box if it makes you feel good! If music isn't a part of your life, try a music app like Pandora. You give the program a few song titles, artists, or genres that you like, and it finds current music it thinks will appeal to you. Imagine the points you'll score with the teenagers in your life if you suddenly drop the name of a popular artist whose music they have no idea you're aware of. I wonder if William Congreve was in the middle of packing up his home when he wrote, "Music has charms to soothe a savage beast." OK, I'm stretching it, but do consider some dulcet tones to make your journey easier or at least more pleasant.

As bathroom and bedroom are intertwined, this week we tackle the lotions, potions, and ragged towels that dog most folks. We sometimes hold on to old sheets, towels, bathroom rugs, and curtains because we want to be thrifty. When they start to look tattered and torn, however, it's time to let them go. A move is a wonderful opportunity to buy towels and linens that fit the new decor. If you bathe a dog at home, you can now dedicate some of those old towels to Fido. I have a special stash set aside just for Charlie. Many of these items can be cut into cleaning rags. I use old towels to cover my birdcages on cold winter nights. Shabby isn't always chic. In addition, this week we open our minds to micro-living. Everything old is new again, and the current generation is creating new riffs on an old life choice.

Shaving the Excess: Packing the Master Bath

The bathroom is part of the master suite, and this week we begin by cleaning out the master bath. You can use these questions in all the bathrooms of your home in the event you are lucky enough to have multiples.

- Does the medicine cabinet contain expired prescription drugs? Do not pour them down the drain or flush them down the toilet—you'll be putting controlled substances into the water supply. To dispose of these medications, grind up pills and mix with coffee grounds, then place in the garbage in a sealed bag to keep the critters in your hood safe. You can also ask your pharmacist if he'll dispose of them. He or she will probably direct you to a mail-in program that costs a few dollars. In some communities the local police department helps with disposal of some prescription medications by supplying a locked drop box. You'll have to contact your precinct to see what programs are available in your community. Finally, for the most detailed guidance, check out the instructions provided by the Food and Drug Administration online (www.FDA.gov).

- Nothing lasts forever, including makeup, body and face lotions, powders, deodorants, shampoos, and so forth. If you regret a purchase, don't hesitate to dispose of the product. It's wasting space.

- Are the hamper and trash can going to work in the new space, or will you have to add these items to your shopping list? Will the current items work elsewhere in the new home? If not, please donate them.

- What about the common accoutrements in this room, like the shower curtain, bathmat, shower caddy, bathtub tray, and curtains? You don't want to schlep them to a place where they are going to look odd.

- If you haven't yet checked the towels in your linen closet, start with the ones on display here. Are they faded, frayed, or unsuitable for the next bathroom?

Here are some makeup guidelines direct from my client Sarah Garcia Azad, the former director of product development at Jouer Cosmetics.

Determining the age of your makeup: It is FDA law that all manufactured makeup have a batch code or lot code on or under the label; for tubes this is crimped into the tube crimp. The code is usually three to five digits or letters or both and is a record of when the makeup was produced. Each brand and lab has a different system, but you can call customer service, give them the code, and find the age of the makeup. For example, F61 in Jouer language stands for June-2006–1st batch that month.

Anything SPF, including powders, gloss, lipstick, and foundation: Toss after two years! Most SPF chemicals are good for only two to three years in cosmetics, and you don't want to use anything that has expired. Most SPF products in bottles or tubes have expiration dates; tubes usually have this date crimped into the end of the tube.

Powders such as eye shadow and blush: These last much longer then you'd think. Most are good up to five years, but pigments can change over time or oils used in the powder can dry out, making them chalky and dry. They are not harmful if old. I say, test it on your skin. If it applies nicely, keep it; if not, toss it.

Wax-based products such as lipstick and cream blushes: These tend to have a nice long shelf life, I'd say often three to five years. Same advice. Test it. Some formulas dry out and get clumpy.

Wet lip gloss and liquid foundations: These should be tossed after one to two years. The ingredients often start to separate. You don't want to allow your skin to absorb old ingredients.

Mascara: If it's used and older than six months, toss it. If still sealed, it can last a few years on the shelf.

This traditionally crowded room should be easy to clean out, but we tend to get emotional about it—perhaps because it can very often be full of our "mistakes." You go to a big-box store and buy two ginormous bottles of shampoo. You've seen the ads on TV and are convinced you'll have supermodel hair after just one application. Unfortunately the product flattens your hair or doesn't smell too inviting, and now you feel stuck with these bottles. Or maybe it's that makeup you saw on the latest Victoria's Secret model that made you look like a character in a zombie movie. You get the idea. Why not offer these mistakes to a girlfriend. They may work wonders for her. After all, they do work for someone, right? Or take unopened products to a local women's shelter. Or (and this is probably my favorite solution because there's a move on the horizon) go crazy and toss it all in the trash. By keeping something you don't like, you're creating a monument to a (well-intentioned) mistake. Remember the quote that opens this chapter? The mistake has taught you that a particular brand doesn't work for you or that certain colors aren't right for your complexion. Isn't that useful information? You really make matters worse when you deny yourself physical space, which I like to think of as a valuable commodity, like food, time, or money. You want to use them not waste them.

The Home Medicine Kit

Medications for gas, indigestion, colds, cuts, bruises, sunburns, and so forth, are usually found in three areas of the home: the master bathroom, the kitchen, and sometimes the guest bathroom near the front door (as opposed to one attached to a guest room). Now is a great time to check the expiration dates of all these products. This usually whittles the collection down by almost half! Combine open bottles of the same product, and toss the empty container(s).

Next you want to categorize: cold, flu, and cough remedies can stay together; everyday items like aspirin, Beano, Preparation H, and Band-Aids can live in another container, and if you have young children, you probably have wraps for sprains and possible breaks (while you are en route to the emergency room). I don't need to rifle through cough remedies when I have a headache, right? I trust you keep your prescription drugs in your medicine cabinet. Grid Totes are great for holding items in these categories. If you are tossing some Rx bottles, be sure to remove the label. We don't want the trash sifters of the world trying to renew your Oxycontin, do we?

Once you create your categories, decide where to keep your stashes. The disposition will depend on how many people are in the home. Older children will want to know where the cold remedies are located, while the toddlers need you to distribute the doses. If you have multiples of some items, create a container of backup products that you check first before you hit the store. I worked with clients recently who were flabbergasted when, on cleaning out their medication stash, they found that a full 75 percent of it had expired. Having a lot of "stuff" in any category often represents what I call "fake prosperity." We feel a false sense of well-being when we gaze into our closet bulging with clothing (we no longer wear), at our overflowing stash of (mostly expired) medicines, or onto our endless sea of cosmetics (most of which are too old to use). In reality, very little of this stuff actually serves us. Let's get real in the next location and know exactly what's in the home in every area. Organizing everyday meds and first aid supplies for the home is a great way to practice the principles in order to experience how good the whittling-down process feels. If you don't have any Grid Totes or don't want to buy them, use old shoeboxes that are in good condition. Some folks decorate them with contact or wrapping paper. I can't imagine expending the time or energy to do that, but if it makes you happy, you'll certainly be creating a bit of beauty in your world. Set this task aside for when you're in the new home, however. Just this sort of project beckons when we unconsciously want to avoid the real work at hand. "Did I pack any boxes today? No. But I made some beautiful storage bins."

Packing Tips for the Bathroom

Filled with a large assortment of nonbreakable items, the master bathroom is fairly easy to box up. I'd pack extra or backup supplies in advance and leave whatever items you use every day until the final week.

Any prescription medicines should stay with you on the day of the move—in either your purse or your bathroom moving-day box. The deciding factor is how critical the drugs are and how quickly you might need them. You don't want to go fishing for life-saving medications while the truck is being unloaded. You have one set of guidelines for a short-haul move and other parameters for a move that will require you to be in transit for several days or longer. The latter will require a larger stash and perhaps a greater variety of items, depending on your health.

Toss small items and open containers (think Q-tips, cotton balls, and floss) into gallon Ziploc bags. Try to pack related categories together as much as possible. Be sure the lids of opened bottles are closed or screwed on tight. You don't want a box to tip, causing something sticky or soapy to coat everything inside it! If you have

Take good care of the movers, because happy movers are less likely to drop or damage your belongings. What makes them happy? A bathroom they can use with plenty of toilet paper, (paper) towels, and soap, as well as coffee in the morning and a plentiful supply of water throughout the day. Go for broke with some morning donuts and a simple lunch. And, of course, the promise of a tip for a job well done.

opened glass bottles, be sure the caps are secure before you pack, and feel free to use towels as cushioning. If you use paper, be generous. Shattered glass in a kitchen box generally means a glass has broken. Shattered glass in a bathroom box suggests some liquid is about to ooze out of the bottom. Ooze is bad enough, but when it's highly perfumed, it's a disaster. By the time you get to this room, you'll be creating categories without thinking about it. You'll be packing boxes that aren't too big, too heavy, or insecure in any way. Practice makes perfect.

Bathroom Moving-Day Box

Think about the items you use every day and have them handy in a medium-size box. Pack as if you were taking a flight. You don't need economy-size bottles of shampoo and conditioner, five blow dryers, and fifteen shades of lipstick. You need to know you can get clean and freshen up. You don't want to look into a mirror and see a person who looks dirty and disheveled because you couldn't find your hygiene products! Include a towel and face cloth. If you store all medications and first aid supplies in the master bathroom, then follow my instructions at the end of the kitchen chapter for these items. And please don't forget to have a few rolls of toilet paper handy! If you have a guest bathroom, designate it for the movers' use and set them up with a few rolls, along with some (paper) towels and soap. Just knowing everyone involved has those supplies handy can preserve peace on moving day.

Planning for the Next Bathroom

If you gain a bathroom, how lucky you will be! There's nothing like sending guests off to their own bathroom, whether they are around for a meal or a weekend. This is a great space to store the toilet paper stash for your home and extra towels. If you have a walk-in pantry, a garage, or a big linen closet, then this bathroom needs only house guest supplies. If you like to entertain, add items in a basket like hair spray, room freshener, aspirin, and a few tampons. You can add or delete items for guests who are making more than a quick visit. If you have sample sizes from first-class travel, use them here or donate them to a shelter. If you work in a large company with lots of traveling executives, you might put out a periodic call for those kits. They make a lovely and practical donation.

The big question, of course, is whether you are gaining or losing space in the master bathroom. Do you have room for a hamper? If not, be sure there's one in each bedroom. If you want towels used more than once, make sure there's a hook or a bar so they can dry between showers or baths. Extra towel bars or hooks almost always help you maximize space. Drawer liner, drawer organizers, and perhaps a few Grid Totes are all great additions to this room. Now that you have downsized your stash, look at what remains and consider the layout of the new bathroom and the number and size of the drawers.

If you are a large family and this is the only bathroom, you may want to have all members keep their towels and bathroom products in their rooms. When each person comes in to bathe, for example, he or she will bring a Grid Tote with supplies and towel. Towels can dry on hooks in bedrooms, and the Grid Totes can live in the bedroom closets. There's always a way to maximize space. Sometimes the solution doesn't involve crowding the space so that everyone who uses it has immediate access to what he or she intends to use. Carrying a Grid Tote when you're off for a shower isn't the most fun in the world, but it's also not the worst punishment.

Perhaps no room more dramatically demonstrates that there are few hard-and-fast rules when it comes to organizing a space. You can be unpredictable, creative, and come up with unique solutions. If you are creating a system, be sure you communicate clearly how it's all supposed to work. And take into account the desires and opinions of all family members. You may not be able to give everyone what he or she wants, but you can give everyone the gift of being heard.

A lack of communication can complicate second marriages, especially when children are involved. As humans, we frequently presume that our way is the right and only way to perform a task. It's important to discuss mundane things, like how you will do the laundry or load the dishwasher. Whose good china will you use on big holidays? The road to relationship hell is paved with assumptions. I like to say that communication, commitment, and compromise will save any day.

A client of mine married a guy who insisted on keeping all of his kitchen tools, even when her microwave, coffeemaker, and vacuum cleaner were more up to date. He never asked what anyone wanted from the grocery store. He brought home what he liked and what he had seen in her pantry before they got married, so unwanted food kept reappearing. It was an upsetting situation that compromise, had he been willing, and communication as a family unit could have resolved. If you want everything your way, you should probably stay single.

If your move involves merging two established homes into one household, be certain you discuss every detail as there's no point in bringing to the new destination a lot of excess items that have to be donated or sold right after you finish fighting about their fate. Hold planning sessions at each other's places. Take the measurements of the new space and all of your furniture. Create a visual that reflects your new life as a couple. You are moving from "I" to "we." If you don't feel you need or want to do this planning, you can continue to visit each other's homes and be married to your stuff. And, yes, the couple referenced above divorced.

The Linen Closet

This is the perfect time to clean out your linen closet. We seem to go on automatic pilot when it comes to bedding and towels. We don't see that they are faded, frayed, no longer absorbent, or threadbare. Sort through your stash and donate discards to the local animal hospital, which will be hugely grateful to have these items. As an animal advocate, I repeat this tip every chance I get.

Very few people are going to fold as beautifully as Martha Stewart. If you have a large family, assign individuals shelves or sections of shelves in the new linen closet and use shelf dividers to keep everyone's items separate. Putting sheets inside a pillowcase keeps together everything a young person responsible for changing his or her linens needs. It's not the prettiest visual, but it teaches the power of categories in a simple way.

If you have a large linen closet and older children, you might want to keep Grid Totes with common remedies and cold and flu relief here. The linen closet is usually in the hall, and an ill person won't have to wait for another family member to finish up in the bathroom or knock on your door and interrupt your privacy or sleep.

Rightsizing Lessons from the Micro-Living Movement

You will have noticed by now that the average move involves a bit of downsizing, and many require a Herculean effort in this department. Over the years I've divested myself of possessions I was once certain would accompany me to my grave. As they have been donated to charity, given to friends, sold, or simply tossed, I have never once experienced regret. Instead I have in every instance been flooded with a sense of peace, freedom, and appreciation for the space acquired.

As you contemplate rightsizing in the weeks ahead, remember that we are not our possessions. They simply reflect who we are at a particular moment. I'm not suggesting a wholesale, unemotional tossing of everything you hold dear. I am reminding you that your life is not made more valuable by the stuff you own—unless, of course, you happen to have a Picasso and a Monet, but then, we won't be downsizing those, will we?

Several related movements in the United States aim to help us see the beauty of "less is more" in our living spaces and the things we stuff into them, and they can offer some inspiration and valuable wisdom for your move or rightsizing project. For too long we have embraced the frenzied and erroneous belief that "more is better." But lately you can find more and more examples of people choosing to live in tiny spaces: micro-houses and -apartments, apartments built inside storage units and freight containers, modular living spaces, and the like. I wonder if living in less than 350 square feet is the wave of the future?

Everything old is new again: one can see variations on this style of micro-living throughout history. At gold rush development sites, temporary workers lived in bare-bones structures as a group, caring little for luxuries like fine china or cut crystal. In the 1940s and 1950s, people rented rooms in rooming houses in Manhattan, preferably at a classy address, and enjoyed all the amenities of the neighborhood. They shared a bathroom with other tenants and either ate with them or had their meals out. Every rooming house had rules, and many prohibited guests, especially of the opposite sex, who might be tempted to spend the night. In big cities, young women who came to get better-paying jobs and send money home to mom and dad lived in women's residences. These continued well into the 1970s. Today in Seattle, community-style living arrangements are popular as recent grads in the tech industry come to forge a career.

Micro-apartments with less than 350 square feet are now being offered in San Francisco, Seattle, and New York City. If they are as successful as expected, builders in other cities will follow suit. The Japanese have elegantly demonstrated that less is more for centuries. I'm not convinced the average American will adopt micro-living, but it's worth considering as an option for an undergraduate's first apartment or the retired empty-nester who wants to devote herself to travel. What about a parent securing a temporary work assignment in a city too far for a daily commute? What if dad wants to live near his children, and mom has been awarded the family home in a divorce? A micro-apartment is an absolute boon in many scenarios. A micro-house might be the perfect guest quarters if you have the property. You could use one as a writing, painting, or dance studio. If you live in a college town, you might rent one to a student. If you go to a city like New York a few times a year, renting a micro-apartment might be cheaper than staying in a hotel. I have a client who converted her garage into a studio apartment so her teenagers had a hangout. See what I mean? You may have recoiled at the very idea of 350 square feet of living space, and now you see it has unforeseen possibilities. Who doesn't want guests to stay outside the home? Who wouldn't want a private space to write, paint, or do crafts? You may believe that for you more space and stuff are the way to go and yet find yourself enchanted by the concept of less—a lot less.

Community-style micro-living remains the exception, not the rule. The prosperity boom after World War II engendered the American dream of individual home ownership. Home sizes ballooned over the ensuing decades. Today a typical American home is twenty-three hundred square feet—twice the size of the typical French home and three times larger than the typical Brit's. When I organize a client who lives in a home built in the early part of the last century, we marvel at the size of the closets. Clearly people didn't have the vast wardrobes now considered normal. The kitchens don't have nearly enough cabinet space for today's supplies, and the garages can barely hold a sedan let alone an SUV. Again and again we return to the question, What is the right size? Clearly, your home's right size is specific to your needs, but we should make conscious decisions about it rather than endlessly acquiring new things or keeping more than we use. Balance is always the goal in any endeavor, especially the quest to be Zen Organized. While it would be difficult to raise a family in less than 350 square feet, for people from all walks of life that size home is an answer to a prayer.

Even if you aren't quite ready to drop everything and move into a 350-square-foot apartment, you can still adapt rather than adopt elements of the micro-solution. You can employ some of the savvy organization and storage tactics that make these small living spaces such a wonder—even if you're still in a larger home.

Here are some basics for small-space living or just making the most of the space you have:

- Hide key items in plain sight. Get a Murphy bed for your sleeping area, and keep the bed folded up when you're not using it. If you're designing a space from scratch, you might add a sleeping loft or purchase a loft bed. For the work or living area, try a writing desk that attaches to the wall. When the desk leaf drops down, a cutout wall section stores paper or books. The desk can also double as a dining table.

- Use furniture that serves multiple purposes. Instead of a traditional coffee table, for example, use an old steamer trunk. You'll have a conversation piece and storage. Or use a contemporary design that has room for storage baskets under the table surface.

- If you have no hall closet, think outside the box: put up hooks or get a narrow coat tree.

- Live paperless and use a laptop you can put away when it's not in use. Consider whether a printer is absolutely necessary—

many UPS and office-supply stores offer reasonable prices to print, so if you don't use yours often, perhaps it's not needed. I used to have an ink-jet printer that produced high-quality color copies and a laser copier for quick black-and-white copies. When I moved I downsized both out of my life, and guess what: I don't miss them at all! The trees love me.

- In a small space you lose storage, so trips to big-box stores for enough toilet paper, paper towels, and napkins to last a year go out the window. You either buy in smaller quantities or go to the big-box store but split your purchases with friends.

- Use smaller kitchen appliances, and leave the sub-zero freezer for the chateau. Install a single-basin sink in a small kitchen and a pedestal sink in the bathroom.

- Install bars on kitchen walls, and hang cooking tools (including pots and pans) from S-hooks. A magnetic knife board will save counter or drawer space.

- Reserve limited cupboard space for glasses, dishes, and serving pieces.

- Attach a wine glass or mug holder to the bottom of a cabinet.

- A tiny kitchen doesn't need a door. If the space is open to the rest of the living space, it will all feel bigger and flow better.

- With a small portable file caddy and a laptop, your office becomes mobile. Plop a lamp on a rattan file box that you don't access often.

- A designer can create pieces of furniture that move and change the layout of the room. A large floor-to-ceiling bookcase can be part of the decor by day but move in the evening to reveal a bedroom area.

You'll find lots of images to spark small-size living ideas at design sites like Houzz.com or the ever-visual Pinterest.com. Check out the books available on the topic at Amazon or a local bookstore or library. Living like this means you are not going to have a huge wardrobe, a vast book or memorabilia collection, or a large crafts workshop. It's not for everyone. But it is the ultimate in pared-down, Zen-like living for those who prefer to use stuff rather than become attached to it. If you intend to raise a large family, you'll want more space. But when the kids have left the nest, you can return to "dorm-style" living. Imagine how free you'll be to travel. Think of how little time, energy, and money you'll spend on maintenance. Consider how you'll reduce your carbon footprint. Many retired couples travel in tricked-out homes on wheels or live on boats docked in local marinas. Small-size living has been around for years, but now we're saying it's not reserved for that weekend cabin in the woods; it's for the way we do life. I am suggesting that you at least consider aspects of it. I love large homes, but even they don't need to be stacked to the rafters. You really aren't your stuff. You are free to identify yourself with the gift of space. With an open mind and a little research, you'll discover the right-size home and the right amount of stuff for your current leg in the journey of life.

Are You a Minimalist?

For the most part, we live in a "more is better" culture—we love to have more, newer things. I enter homes where every family member owns an iPad, and if it's lost, a new one has arrived by nightfall. When a child turns sixteen and gets a learner's permit, he or she is given a new vehicle. Big-screen TVs, replaced by the latest flat screen, languish in the garage. Clothing is purchased and worn once or forgotten. I've taken carloads of items with the tags still on to Goodwill. We keep up with the proverbial Joneses and savor the high from a shopping spree. Seldom do we take a moment to realize the nuttiness of this scenario, which in no way feeds our souls.

Adopting minimalist principles might just offer a meaningful alternative. In *Minimalism: Live a Meaningful Life*, Joshua Fields Millburn and Ryan Nicodemus outline their minimalist philosophy. A period of loss and difficulty forced them to ask themselves what was truly important. Eschewing corporate success, big houses, and expensive stuff as paths to fulfillment, they embrace less while concentrating on five major aspects of life: health, relationships, passion, growth, and contribution.

There's also the 2013 documentary *Tiny: A Story About Living Small*, in which filmmaker Christopher Smith decides to put down roots and build a tiny home just before his thirtieth birthday—despite having never built anything like it before. In addition to Christopher and his girlfriend, the film introduces six other tiny-house dwellers who stripped down to explore a different meaning of "home" and the value of living with less.

You may not totally embrace minimalism, but you might choose to adopt aspects of it into your present lifestyle. It's worth considering whether you could indeed be happy with less while having more in

When planning a move, many of us would like to chuck what we own and start fresh in a new apartment or home. Few of us have those resources, but that doesn't mean we are limited in our ability to express ourselves differently in a new space. Never underestimate the power of paint. You don't have to do an entire room in an eye-catching color; you can do one wall as a dramatic accent. I just discovered chalkboard paint and find it's a lot of fun in the kitchen or in a child's room. You can also rotate your decorative pieces with the seasons. People will suspect you have done some major redecorating when you just changed the items on the coffee table. Ideas abound at sites like Pinterest and Houzz. Take some time to see how creative you can be on a shoestring budget.

other areas outside your current focus. What have you got to lose but that technological graveyard in the garage, a pile of rarely worn clothing, too much weight around your middle, or a five-thousand-square-foot home when eighteen hundred would make you much happier?

Week's Summary

- ❑ Downsize the contents of all bathrooms.
- ❑ Pack whatever items you won't need until you get to the new location, including linens.
- ❑ Clean out the linen closet, and donate discards to your vet or local emergency animal hospital.
- ❑ Consider the benefits and how-tos of micro-living.

A Closing Thought

We've all walked into homes or public spaces and been instantly uncomfortable. We are responding to the energy of the place. By now the energy in your current residence must be feeling "lighter." Yes, you have a growing sea of boxes, but you also have a steady march out the door of items you can toss or donate. Right about now you may get what I call "the fever." My clients get toss happy and feel everything can go. They start to work into the wee hours because they want to accelerate the process. Slow down. Rome wasn't built in a day; nor did you fill up this home in a weekend. Give yourself the gift of the remaining weeks. You're halfway there, and excitement should be growing. The best reward you can give yourself as this week comes to a close is a few extra hours of sleep. Nothing will refresh and restore you faster. Next week we're going to tackle paper. I need you to be as rested as possible. Paper produces anxiety. We need to clear it out and whittle it down so it won't be the same kind of demon in the next location.

THE END OF PAPER PILES

All great changes are preceded by chaos.
—DEEPAK CHOPRA

IT'S AMAZING HOW MUCH POWER WE GIVE PAPER. WE AVOID IT. We save it when it could easily leave us forever. We can't find it when we need it. We invite more into our homes without any direction, and we allow it to create oceans of guilt and shame. Let's leave this behavior behind in the current house or apartment, shall we? Those piles represent wasted time, money, and energy.

Of all the tasks you need to complete before your move, packing up the home office may be the most difficult. It's challenging to write about paper problems because I can't see your personal situation. Are you a mom with a workstation in her kitchen and one drawer of files or an entrepreneur running a home-based business and drowning in an ocean of paper in a dedicated home office? Are you a college student in his first apartment with one cardboard box for files or a retired couple with tax backup material going back decades?

SELF-CARE TIP
FOR THE WEEK

IF YOU MEDITATE on a regular basis, then you are already feeling the benefits during this process. If you have no clue what meditation is or how it's done, or you fear it will open you up to psychological or spiritual disaster, read on. As human beings we never stop thinking, do we? Our heads are filled with nonstop chatter. We're making decisions. We're weighing the benefits of an action. We're judging others' appearances or lifestyles. We're wondering why some members of our family are so difficult to deal with and never see the right way to do anything. The list is endless. This constant babble is exhausting to our system. In Eastern religions meditation has a specific spiritual application. For our purposes, however, I'm not interested in whether or not you believe in God or what your concept of "It" is. I simply want to help you relax.

Here are but a few of the recognized benefits of meditation:

- Relaxed muscles
- Reduced heart rate
- Increased clarity in thinking
- Deeper sleep
- Lower stress-hormone levels
- Increased focus
- Improved memory
- Reduced inflammation in the body (a recognized cause of disease)

I don't think anything on this list will send you screaming into the night. It takes consistent practice to reap the rewards, but that's true of most good habits. Your lungs don't clear an hour after you give up smoking, right? Positive results need to be cultivated. This tool will help you for the rest of your life. Fifteen to thirty minutes a day would be ideal, but if you only have five to start, then that's all you need to commit to.

There are many simple practices. You can sign up online for a course in Transcendental Meditation, which The Beatles made famous in the 1960s. Self-Realization Fellowship (SRF), a trusted organization, has a presence online, temples around the world, and an at-home study course. Mysteries.net provides extraordinary material on the subject (Graham Ledgerwood has been my instructor for over thirty years); you'll also find a home-study course for a nominal fee. Yoga studios have sprouted up all over America, and many offer classes in meditation. The technique I'm sharing with you is simple, effective, ancient, and easy to learn. Are you ready?

Sit in a straight-back chair with your feet flat on the floor. Place your hands on your thighs with your palms facing up. Don't let them touch. (Many people new to meditation find their hands migrating toward each other in their lap. Keep them apart, palms facing up, on your thighs.) Close your eyes and pay attention to your breathing. Breathe normally. Feel your breath as it enters and then exits your nostrils. Do this for five minutes. Think of nothing else but focusing on your breath. When thoughts intrude, gently dismiss them, without judgment or annoyance. And don't be surprised if you fall asleep. All of these things are normal in the beginning. Over time, focusing on your breath will get easier. Don't be shocked if you enjoy the practice and the benefits so much that you decide to increase the time you devote to meditation.

Every time I've suggested meditation to a client, I hear the same thing: "Oh, I can't meditate. I've tried. I simply can't stop thinking." This inability to focus is common to all beginners; it even has a name: "monkey mind." Just as the wild monkey leaps from tree to tree, our mind leaps from thought to thought. The simple exercise above, done with devotion, will over time bring you an exquisite gift. You will experience a quiet mind. In fact, I think it's safe to say that you will always remember the first time it happens. I was meditating in the chapel at the SRF temple in Pacific Palisades after a Sunday service when it happened to me. But let's not have lofty goals for now. I just want for you to feel less exhausted and more focused during this process.

To err on the side of caution, I'll be describing the worst-case scenario. If that doesn't apply to you, I give you permission to gloat and move quickly through all the assignments. You'll need the time you save this week for that part of the home that is your Achilles' heel.

The Paper Demon: Packing the Home Office

Now that we've taken time to focus and reduce some stress, let's turn to the home office and any piles of papers lying around. Paper piles are stacks of unmade decisions. Yes, it's that simple. Why do we avoid making decisions? In general there are three main culprits. First, we fear making a mistake—as if tossing a paper in error is a criminal offense. Second, we have not created a system to catch and hold our paper. Knowing I need a document doesn't tell me where to put it. Third, having put a system in place, we neglect to review and tweak it over time. Imagine a child in the first grade whose mom never edits his wardrobe. Before long, what he needs is missing, and what is present is mostly useless. Paper is the same. Any office or file system should be alive with current information. Otherwise, you have a paper cemetery.

Get Clear of the Fear

If your fear of paper extends to every single piece you touch, you need to do some critical thinking that will enable you to put the phobia to rest. As you make paper-related decisions for the current papers on your desk and in your files, you will build that muscle, and I promise it gets easier over time. Can you identify where the fear originated? Knowing that will put you in a better position to develop a new response. Very often we live with a fear created decades ago without ever realizing that we can now take the sting out of that memory. For example, did you toss a piece of paper that was important and get into trouble with a parent, spouse, or boss? How old were you when that happened? What did you learn from that experience? Would you make that mistake today? Thinking through the emotions that continue to control you will help release them or at least ease their grip on you. Isn't it amazing how we forget compliments but hold on to hurtful remarks for decades? Paper represents, among other things, the business of life, and it's important to be in control of your finances. You need to diffuse this fear, and a move is a powerful motivator.

If you have a paper wizard among your friends or family, ask him or her to help you. If you'd rather work with a stranger, find a professional organizer who specializes in office organization. You can start with the National Association of Professional Organizers (NAPO), a national organization with chapters in all the large cities. But don't make NAPO membership a prerequisite, because lots of talented organizers choose not to join (including yours truly). Interview a few folks and see whose personality meshes best with yours. Organizing is very intimate, and you want to be in skilled hands that are also compatible and fun.

If in your heart of hearts you know you don't want to be bothered with the day-to-day maintenance involved with paperwork, consider hiring someone to set up the system with you and then pay that person to come in once a week or month to do the grunt work. If you run a home-based business, this expense is tax deductible. You can find a college student or, for a tad more money, a retired person with more experience. If you have the means, you can also turn over this aspect of your life to a bookkeeper or accountant. The office where your tax return is prepared may also have part-time or seasonal employees looking for outside work. You needn't feel any shame in asking for help. The paper wizards have fears of their own about other things in life.

Rightsize Your Life Activity: Get Those Papers Sorted!

You want to get those stacks of paper scattered about your office into some kind of order. Here are a few questions to ask as you hold each paper in your hands. If you know instantly that you don't need it, toss it. (I'm using the phrase "toss it," but you can recycle or shred, as each piece suggests.) Sort those you do need to keep into broad categories, such as the following: receipts, home, insurance, legal, medical, projects, recipes, reference, school, sports, travel, and warranties. Place related items in separate stacks on a clear surface like your dining room table. Use Post-it notes to identify each stack so you don't have to pause every few minutes to determine what you had in mind when you started one. We want to speed things along.

I don't want you to get perfectionistic or be overly specific, but the one mistake my clients make when they sort their papers without me is to make a new stack of all the papers they need to keep. I want you to put *related* items together in *separate* stacks or piles. They will go into individual file folders in another phase of this operation. For now I need you to eliminate and categorize.

Here are some questions to help in case you don't have an immediate yes or no for an item.

- Is it related in any way to your taxes? If yes, keeping it is a must. (See "Dispelling Tax Phobia" on page 134 for more on this.)
- Does this paper provide proof of purchase for an item you own? If it's a big-ticket item like a refrigerator, staple the receipt to the warranty or instruction manual. If it's a receipt for,

say, an iron, I would keep it for the length of the guarantee. Set these receipts aside, and at the end of your sorting, do all the stapling at once.

- You will surely come across household bills and expense receipts. Make another pile for them.

- Is the item an article you feel you must read . . . one day? Consider that material is always being recycled in periodicals, and you can find the latest and greatest on any subject on the Internet 24/7. How long have you had this article? If you haven't read it in the last two months, odds are that you won't. Toss it.

- If you just can't bear to lose it, and it's in a newspaper, magazine, or other publication, tear or cut out the article and create a "to read" stack. This will take up a lot less real estate than an entire magazine or newspaper. I cut out newspaper articles, but I just rip magazines pages along the spine rather than bothering with scissors. If it's a long piece, staple the pages together.

- If the article is about something you are working on at home (like a remodel) or a project at work, set it aside. Keep project materials in separate stacks.

- Is this a flyer for a sale that has passed? Toss it. You're on the store's radar, so there will be more invitations in the future.

- If you find invitations, check the date. Did you miss a party? Make a note on your calendar to write the hostess a note or send a belated gift. Put the address in your address book if you don't have it recorded. Toss the invitation. If it's an upcoming event, file it! We'll talk about names for folders in a later section should you need help with that aspect.

- It's OK to toss holiday photos of other people's children. They don't expect you to create an album.

- If you're a parent, you have probably saved numerous examples of your child's artwork. Take photographs and set up a digital album so that everybody you know can watch the evolution of little Johnny's talent. Save the best from each year if you need a hard copy memento, and put it in an artist's portfolio. Remember, you're saving this for you, not little Johnny. I've never met an adult who wanted to have his or her artwork from kindergarten or the first grade. It would be a tad creepy even for the most self-involved among us—unless of course your name is Picasso and you can sell these treasures for millions.

As you sort through the piles on your dining room table and possibly the floor, the feel in the room is going to change. Instead of random piles, you will have stacks of related material, and your recycle bin will be full. This creates space in the room and in your brain. "Stuff" is noisy and impedes our ability to think clearly. I hope you enjoy this growing sense of freedom as you sort and toss.

THE FAMOUS WRITER

I once organized a famous writer who works in a guesthouse behind her home. When I walked in, I was impressed to see lots of filing cabinets. When I opened each drawer to see what system was currently in place, I was shocked to find they were all empty. Stacks and stacks of paper littered every surface of the office. My client assured me she knew what was in every one of them. I knew from experience that was impossible. She might indeed be familiar with what was on top of each, but to remember every item in every stack would have meant she was Superwoman and had X-ray vision.

I made her a deal. We'd go through the stacks, and I would create a file system for her. If she didn't like it, I would return in two weeks and restore the stacks. The only caveat was that she had to really use the system, not just reject it because it was new. After we slogged our way through a few stacks, my client told me that I was right. She not only didn't know what was in a particular stack, she didn't remember most of the stuff and was grateful to find a few treasures. We continued on, and I never had to restore those stacks.

What's in Your Files?

Now is the time for you to examine your files. If you have a system you love, then simply scan all the files in your cabinet or box to see if any material can be cleaned out before the move. If you don't have a system at all, or you have one that doesn't serve you, or you have the typical mishmash, this week we're going to set you on the road to proper paper maintenance. I can't lie and say that filing paper is fun, but it is something of a Zen experience because it's fairly mindless and mechanical. Because time is short, I'm going to suggest an extremely rudimentary version of my typical file system. You can flesh it out at your next location. I'll give you the tips you need and talk about the supplies that will help. But first let's open each drawer in turn and move folder by folder, looking for what can be eliminated. You'll be amazed at the amount of material you have outgrown. It's a fairly universal experience.

More times than I care to count, I open a new client's filing cabinet and can't make heads or tails of the files I find. When I ask about the system in use, I hear that my client has tried several, and the remnants of each are in the drawers. In other words, the file folders provide an illusion of order. It takes a bit of time to establish a file system, but it saves you more time, energy, and money in the long run than you expend setting it up. Let's consider a few simple steps you can take so that you are able to exit this home with a modicum of order.

What is the key to any system? It's your old friend "decision making." Every day paper enters your home in a myriad of ways. You simply can't put off deciding where something will live; otherwise the piles start to grow, and soon just walking into your office depresses you. Some people box up the piles and go for a fresh start. I've had clients who tossed material without looking at it, believing that if they hadn't needed it over the past few weeks, months, or even years, they probably didn't need it at all. Yikes! What if they were tossing their social security card or passport? They are certainly replaceable, but that takes time, wastes money, and robs you of the ability to travel outside the country at a moment's notice. You get the idea.

Separate from individual folders, you may have project files. Ask yourself if you can recycle or shred these papers. Perhaps you ran a fund-raiser for your son's school, and now that he's graduated, your involvement has ended. Why hold on to those papers? If you need to keep a project for reference, put it in a separate location designated for archival files. It could live with your tax backup material, either in another filing cabinet or at the back of a closet. If you are lucky enough to have that extra filing cabinet in your garage, keep archived projects in separate drawers from the tax backup material. As you are going to be tossing one year of taxes each April, you could eyeball your archived project files at the same time. And let me urge you to keep that cabinet locked. A garage is very often left open on a hot summer day while the family wafts in and out of the house. You may also have workmen, a handyman, or your friendly gardener and his crew there at various times. I'm sure they are all honest citizens, but on the off chance one is turned on by identity theft, don't invite yourself to that party.

Myth Buster

This is a good time to dispel a myth in the world of most aspiring organizers. When you read that professional organizers urge you to handle a piece of paper once, that doesn't mean you have to stop what you're doing and perform whatever action each piece of paper demands the minute it arrives. You'll never accomplish anything on your real to-do list because the need to make a phone call, send an e-mail, or dispatch a snail mail item will demand your attention. You need to have a file system in place to absorb each piece of paper in a specific location. When you designate a time to do paperwork, all those collected tasks will be waiting for you. Imagine how easy and effortless dealing with paper will be once you have a place for the contents of every envelope, for every receipt in your purse, for every paper that your child hands you from school, and so forth.

Space Hog

Many of my clients keep warranties and instruction manuals in the filing cabinet; others keeping the information for big-ticket items, like TVs, washers and dryers, and the stove, with that equipment. If that works for you, by all means continue. And if you own the home you're leaving and are not taking some appliances, be sure you pull out those booklets this week so the new occupants can handle house calls as easily as you have. I like to keep all such material together, but not just tossed into a drawer. Good luck finding the item you need. Take a few minutes to sort through your collection. You will be amazed by how many items you no longer own. If some are on their way to a charity or a friend, put the manuals with the item. If you already gave the item away and are now holding the instructions in your hand, don't fret; manuals are now generally accessible at the manufacturer's website. Give it a toss.

When it comes to organizing your collection, think in categories. Put all large kitchen and laundry appliances, like the refrigerator, stove, washer, and dryer, in one file folder and small kitchen appliances, like the KitchenAid mixer and the Cuisinart food processor, in another. Create an "entertainment" file for the booklets for the TVs, DVRs, and so forth. Make another for the office (supplies and furniture) and probably a separate one for computers. If you divide your material in this way, when you need to find something specific, it will be a matter of choosing the right category. I keep my files in alphabetical order, but I usually place warranties in the back of the bottom drawer of a filing cabinet. That's how often I assume they will be needed! Two-inch-wide box-bottom expanding file folders are great for thick files like these.

If you like to read computer instruction manuals (yes, I have some of you as clients), you probably have them on a bookcase shelf in your office along with the original packaging for the software program. I think that's an ideal place because you actually reference the material. You'll want yours on a low shelf. The rest of us mere mortals will store ours on the highest shelf or in the supply closet. Check the years to be sure you're still using that version. Those of us who will never touch a computer manual can toss them and store the discs in a box designed for that purpose and keep that on a bookcase shelf.

Dispelling Tax Phobia: How to File Important Documents

Tax documentation is one of the biggest components of filing. Over the years I've noticed the biggest fear in terms of making a paperwork mistake involves Uncle Sam. The idea of making a mistake on a tax return conjures images of being hauled in for an audit. In reality most mistakes on tax returns are mathematical, and we're either asked for an additional payment or sent a bigger refund. Many of my clients, however, are convinced that, out of the blue, for reasons they can't fathom, they are going to be audited decades from now. If they toss the outdated backup material as I request, they will not be able to substantiate a deduction and will owe a boatload of money. Fear is a powerful force. Let's examine the reality and shed some light on your situation because boxes of old receipts take up room and invite the creepy crawlies who feast on paper.

Uncle Sam has time guidelines for every piece of paper involved in some way on your tax return. The person you pay to prepare your taxes has up-to-date information on those guidelines, assuming he or she is a professional and not your Uncle Sal, who happens to "be good with numbers." If Sal files your return, you need to visit IRS. gov and research the length of time particular documents have to remain in your possession (see page 143). In general it's three years for your federal return if you file as a private citizen and seven if you file as a corporate entity.

Each state sets its own retention period for the state return documentation. I live in California, and for residents of the Golden State, it's four years. Every year, when I box up the receipts for the year I just filed, I shred all of the documents from four years before. It's a painless process that keeps me from being overrun by paper; at the same time, I can put my hands on whatever I need if a tax question should arise. If Uncle Sal doesn't know the state retention laws, you can call your state representative's office for the latest guidelines. Or you can google "tax office" with the name of your state. Be sure you let Uncle Sal know how clever you are!

If you cheat on your taxes and hide income or commit any other type of fraud, there is no statute of limitation. Uncle Sam can go back decades and request paper documentation. What are the odds this applies to your situation? I would guess the correct response is slim to none. You do want to hold on to your return forever. Why? Because Uncle Sam sometimes loses them, and if you don't have proof that you filed, you will indeed be liable for your tax bill all over again. Yes, it happens. Ask the professional who prepares your return. I learned this tidbit from the woman who prepares mine. It's best to store them in a fireproof metal box.

Most returns now are filed electronically, so the lines at the post office are dwindling on April 15. It's fairly easy to make digital copies of most of the backup material, so storage space in the home for coming generations will be less. Remember that wasted space is just that, whether in your filing cabinet or on your computer, a jump drive, or the Cloud. Making decisions is a powerful process and will spread to all aspects of your life. You may even enjoy it once you realize that you have the power when you are the decision maker. Resist the temptation to scan every unimportant receipt and keep it forever just because you can. This is akin to never taking out the trash. I rest my case.

If you hoard old tax material, you first need to call your tax pro or the IRS to find out what guidelines apply to you. We need to move quickly, because going through old receipts can really suck up your valuable time. A receipt from ten years ago may remind you of that great house painter you used, but the three hours you spend trolling through the box of decade-old receipts could be spent getting this room ready for your move. Have this material professionally shredded if it's more than one box. It's costly if the company sends someone to you but really cheap if you deliver the materials. You can even watch your material go into the giant shredder these companies use. Find one that is licensed and bonded. You can google your area, check the phone book, or ask a colleague for a reference. Large office-supply stores charge about $1 per pound.

I grew up in New York City, and we didn't have a car most years. If you have no way to transport boxes, find a service that will do the shredding in a truck sent to your address. I know you want to watch, don't you? Be sure you deduct this expense next year when you file if you run a business from home. It's a legitimate office expense. If neither of these solutions appeals or is available to you (let's say you live in a rural area far from a city), you might want to do the shredding yourself. I would toss or recycle the papers with no information that an identity thief might use and shred a few pages of the remaining papers every time you walk into and out of your home office. Have you ever used a shredder for a concentrated period? I can't tell you how many I've jammed or burned up. It's never efficient. Which papers will you shred by hand? The ones with your social security, bank account, and credit card account numbers or any series of numbers that identifies you legally or financially. This can be a great task for older children or teens who want to make a little extra money. Pay for the project not by the hour!

I once worked with a client whose husband owned the business. She was dedicated to the company but was incapacitated with fear about paper. She wouldn't part with anything. Not a single piece of paper elicited an OK to toss from her, and each no took several minutes. It was excruciating and expensive! Job security can work against you, can't it? Fortunately the company had a huge physical space with the money for additional off-site storage. If she had sent her actual trash to be stored, everyone would be up in arms, right? In fact, all across the country people are paying good money to store unneeded paper, and that is a form of trash. Even if you are very wealthy and money is no object, consider how much good those monthly rental checks could be doing in the world to help suffering humans and animals. It's a thought.

Here's a list of some documentation you will want to keep for a specific period, provided it represents expenses you deduct on your returns:

- Investment papers that confirm the purchase, sale, or transfer of your holdings
- Pay stubs
- Financial statements, including those from your broker, mutual funds, 401(k), and all other retirement plans, as well as your children's college-savings plans
- Bank statements (which the IRS can check for income you may have neglected to declare)
- Credit card statements (if they include purchases for which you have no other receipts)
- Utility and phone bills, if they are deductible (which they could be if you run a home-based business)

Here's a list of some documentation you can feel free to shred:

- Credit card statements if the purchases are solely personal and not deductible. Shred them after your payment has been credited. If there is a purchase dispute, hold on to the statement until it is resolved. And remember that statements are available online for up to a year or more with most financial institutions.
- Utility and phone bills if these are not deductible. Shred them after you see that your payment has been credited.
- ATM receipts and deposit slips. These can be shredded after you reconcile your bank statements.
- Any paperwork that duplicates files you have safely stored online. You can always generate a printout if you need one.

I have to add one caveat. This advice is from Julian Block, a tax attorney based in Larchmont, New York. Block advised financial planner Russell Wild and me when we wrote *One Year to an Organized Financial Life*, where much of the above first appeared. Block pointed out that some tax-related documentation is outside the conventional time guidelines and needs to be kept until it no longer affects future returns. This type of documentation includes any showing the purchase price for stocks, mutual funds, real estate, or other investments. Audits aside, these documents will help you figure your profits and losses on sales that may not take place for many years.

Rightsize Your Life Activity: Clear Tax Debris

If bells and whistles are going off in your head and you realize that you have held on to tax documentation for decades unnecessarily, your assignment is to clear that debris. For the years you do need to save, don't bother sorting receipts into categories. Simply keep individual years separate. You want to have categories of receipts going forward, but the past doesn't need your detailed attention. Keep everything bundled together by year. Large brown envelopes are a great way to store the material. In the event you are audited, you can sort those receipts before your appointment. It's highly unlikely this task will ever fall to you.

I like to see these records stored in a locking filing cabinet because they contain juicy identity theft material. The ideal spot would be in your home office, and the secondary spot would be your garage. Designate one place for the key that unlocks the cabinet, and be sure your partner knows where that is. (In the event of an emergency, you don't want to have to call a locksmith.) If you have no space for a filing cabinet dedicated to archival material, put it in file boxes you can easily obtain from a big-box office-supply store, unless of course your mover left you with a few. I would label these boxes with a code rather than something like "Income Tax Records" and indicate the year. I'm sure your movers are honorable, but I like to avoid temptation at all costs. Tuck these boxes in the back of your office closet. Lacking that resource, use the back of your hall, guest room, or master bedroom closet. Tape them shut.

Take Stock

With so much information tossed, ready for shredding, or archived, you should now be surrounded by the active material to put in files for your reference. Having receipts sorted prior to tax time makes tax prep easier than if you just dump every receipt into a box. You won't be surprised to learn I have clients who do just that because they have bookkeepers who sort it all for them. If you can afford that luxury, that's one way to go. If you are incapable of paying your bills on time, turn the task over to an accountant or bookkeeper. That expense is cheaper than the thousands more you will pay in interest every time you wish to purchase a big-ticket item like a car, house, or big-screen TV when your trashed FICO score surfaces. Just be sure you sign the checks. Never allow another entity, no matter how trustworthy, to sign for you. Oprah doesn't! I've had hard-working clients (think surgeons, attorneys, or directors) who simply couldn't be bothered with bill paying when they got home. You aren't a better person if you do your own paperwork.

Many of you pay your bills online, and that is another great choice. Most companies will send you a reminder e-mail as the due date approaches. If you set up automatic payments, please remember to log them in your check register lest your account balance reflect a fantasy rather than what is actually available. Why am I talking about bill paying in a book about moving? Because moving can make you crazy with the additional tasks it adds to your schedule, and bill pay-ing can easily slip though the cracks. I'm an advocate for a great FICO score.

Paper Sorting Before a Move: The Down and Dirty Method

I assume you have a move on the horizon and making beautiful files isn't a top priority. I've come up with a way for you to keep everything categorized and easy to find. At the other end you can fine-tune the system. I know I couldn't wait for the unpacking to be done so that life would feel normal again. Setting up a great file system will seem like a picnic after what you've been through.

Remember when I asked you to sort your papers and gave you a list of potential categories? Please look at the categories you created and make a list on a sheet of paper. Let's say you come up with something like this:

Home
Medical
Projects
    Move
    Remodel at New Home
    Trip Home for the Christmas Holidays
Reference Material
Tax Documents
Warranties

You may have noticed that I alphabetized this list, down to the specific projects I listed under the heading "Projects." You can purchase box-bottom hanging file folders (two inches wide) and put your categories in these until your move is complete. You should purchase one bag of extra-long file tabs and create labels that identify the contents. I'd prefer you do this with a label maker. You don't have to buy the top-of-the-line machine. It's a basic organizing tool that can be used all over the home. Sign up for points or perks at your local big-box office-supply store, and you might earn enough credits to get one free. That's how I got one for my assistant.

Many professional organizers will tell you to make a folder for every important topic and simply file them in alphabetical order. I like to keep related files together. I think it saves time and makes you more powerful. I had a client whose files were done in the more traditional manner. She had several banks of filing cabinets. Carol was in the medical field and licensed to practice in several states. This meant that regulations for California, Hawaii, Nevada, and New Mexico were in separate file folders in various cabinets. I suggested she bring all the file folders together in one box-bottom hanging file folder labeled "Health Care: The States." If you agree that this would work well for you, go ahead and keep categories together when you set up your fleshed-out system.

If you are truly a "I hate file folders" kind of person, then use the same strategy to divide and organize your materials but put them in binders. You can devote a binder to a specific large and growing category like a home remodel or have a big binder with multiple tabs for a complex category like household expenses. Each tabbed section is the equivalent of a file folder. Keep your binders handy and be sure to put a label on the spine. Feel free to use color to identify special projects.

Building a Permanent Filing System: The Real Deal

You have taken a step in the right direction in terms of getting organized. Everybody needs to have a file system. Set up to mirror the needs of your life, it will expand and contract with you over time. If you are a digital person, you can use the same guidelines. The difference is, you don't have to stop at Staples for a box of manila folders because your folders are on the computer. Be sure you have automatic backup in place, in addition to the Cloud. It isn't a question of whether or not your computer will crash but rather when. Better safe than sorry.

When you're ready to develop a more inspired file system, you'll break these categories into the parts they contain. Let me give you a few examples. Let's consider tax documents. What might I find here? All the material that corroborates the deductions you'll claim on your next tax return. I work at home and can deduct a portion of my rent and utilities. I drive to see my clients, so I can deduct a portion of my lease payment, the amount I spend on gasoline, and any repairs. You get the idea. My files look something like this in terms of tax-related material for business expenses:

Business Expenses (add current year)
    Automobile (Gas, Lease, Registration, Repairs)
    Business Entertaining
    Business Gifts
    Business Travel
    Income
    Phones (Land Line and Cell)
    Rent and Utilities (Electric and Gas)

"Business Expenses" is the name of the section, and it's on a long tab on a hanging file folder. It visually announces that the files that follow all relate to that category. You see the individual names here, and each would be on a file folder so that I have a safe place to collect every receipt until I do my taxes. The next file tab will announce a new category. You can break down every project into the aspects that create the whole, just as I did with "Business Expenses." For example, let's say you have been remodeling your new home before you move in. A remodel is a big undertaking, with myriad paperwork and an army of professionals helping you. You might create something along these lines:

Remodel
   Architect
   Budget/Bank Loan
   Contractor
   Permits

Whenever you look at a stack of papers that you have identified as part of one project or topic, you will find there are subdivisions within that whole. You don't want to have to look at building permits and your bank loan, when all you need is the contract you signed with your architect. In the same way I don't want to rifle through phone bills and medical bills when I have to add up business travel receipts. Just a little bit of thought at the start of a project puts you in a position of strength. It's like laying a good foundation before you put up the frame of a house. You can skip the foundation, but don't expect the house to last over time.

Action Files

In the front of any file system, whether it's stripped down or complex, you should have a section called "Action Files." I would have some fun with these and use the color red, which suggests action. Here you will file your tasks. As you open your mail, you should be near your action files and have a cross-cut shredder, trash can, or recycle bin handy. I suggest the following headings:

To Do: ASAP
To Do: Low Priority
To File
To Read

You can separate your to-do items into "To Do: ASAP" and "To Do: Low Priority." This may also bring you some mental relief because your to-do folder won't be quite so full. As you complete items in your to-do folder, you can file them in their appropriate permanent file homes or in a wonderful file called "Pending." For example, if a medical bill has been paid and submitted to my insurance carrier, I no longer want it in my to-do folder, right? I'm simply waiting for reimbursement. Sometimes before you can come to a conclusion, you need to receive a piece of paper from another person or corporate entity. You want to check your to-do file regularly, but who wants to see paper that has been handled? Add a "Pending" file. Voila! I check mine once a week to see if an item has been resolved and can be filed or if perhaps I need to goose someone. In that case it remains in Pending, waiting for resolution.

Office Organizing Tools

Every good organizing system has specific tools that make it sing. Many of you will have some or all of these supplies in your home already. There's nothing costly or exotic. It's pretty run-of-the-mill stuff and easy to find. The most expensive items are probably the box-bottom hanging file folders, cross-cut shredder, and label maker, and you probably have at least one of these already.

- Box-bottom folders come twenty-five to a box and can be used in concert with the more popular individual hanging file folder. Think of them as an additional tool, not as a replacement for the single hanging file folder you are used to using. Box-bottoms save space and enable you to keep an entire category of material together. I suggest no wider than two inches because after that they get too clunky and tend to tear.

- While you're at the big-box office-supply store (or shopping online), pick up a cross-cut shredder if you don't have one. It's your best defense in the identity-theft wars. You can develop the shred habit and won't know how you ever lived without one.

- If you don't have a label maker, you will never regret purchasing one. You can use it all over the house. All the major brands are about the same in quality, so get a simple one for about $30 or less if there's a sale or you have "store money" earned from previous purchases. If something happens to you or you need to ask someone to find an important paper on your behalf, you want others to be able to read the folder tabs easily. My handwriting leaves everything to be desired, so I take my own advice. In fact, I can't even read it most days and would be lost without my trusty label maker.

- A box of manila file folders with either a straight or a one-third cut will give you a wider space for a label, and more space gives you an opportunity to be precise and creative. I want to eliminate the phrase "What did I call that file?" Staggered tabs seem like a good idea until you remove or add folders and suddenly you have a zigzag visual and feel a little queasy every time you search for a file folder. If you have several projects, you might want to invest in colored file folders to distinguish each one. Manila is great for the mundane business of life.

- Get one box of regular hanging file folders. These hang in the cabinet on rails, and you put the manila or colored folder inside. If your cabinet is set for legal-size hanging file folders, and you can't adjust the configuration in the drawer, your hanging files will have to be legal. If your paper stash is all letter-size, however, don't hesitate to use letter-size folders.

- Pick up a bag of extra-long file tabs. These attach to the hanging file folder. You'll get a bag of short tabs with your file folder purchase, but I personally never use them. A longer tab gives you more room to be creative and describe what's on the manila folder(s) you place inside.

- The average person needs a two- to four-drawer filing cabinet, but you can pick that up at the new house. You'll certainly find them at the big-box stores, or you can peruse sites like Craigslist.org or Freecycle.org to see if you can score a deal. If you have a filing cabinet, ask the movers if it's OK to leave your files inside the drawers. Some movers will be comfortable with that; others will want you to empty the cabinet. If you have to pack the files, dedicate a box to the contents of each drawer, and label it clearly. You can fill in any empty space with books or magazines from your office.

- Not everyone likes filing cabinets because of their utilitarian look. You can find file boxes in materials like wood or rattan that fit seamlessly into your decor. If you are moving to a studio, for example, you can set a lamp on your fancy file storage box, and no one will be the wiser—unless of course that's the very one they use at home. Lately I've seen file cabinets in designer colors, so if a fire engine red cabinet would be your dream come true, I think you're in luck.

- Be sure to use surge protectors. It's a modest expense that provides comfort in the event of an electrical mishap in your system.

- Establish a charging station for your cellphone(s), MP3 player(s), and tablet(s). We used to wander around our homes in search of our keys. Now we wander like the lost tribes of Israel in search of our chargers, cellphones, and remotes. The idea of assigning every item a place was never more powerful than with our electronic devices.

Some of my clients ask why they need a manila folder to go inside the hanging file folder. Can't they just put the material in the hanging file folder and save a tree? Here's the potential nightmare: you need material from several files on your desk today. You remove the material and place it all in neat stacks. We humans get a bit careless as we get busy, so in short order the material starts to blend together as if you were mixing ingredients for a cake. At the end of the day, you have to resort the paper before you can put it away. If you're tired, you might put that task off until the next day. Eventually, you have a mess on your desk as if you had never taken the time to get organized. Manila folders are inexpensive and help you stay organized as they keep your categorized papers in one tidy location. You can, of course, go crazy and purchase folders with fancy designs or in color, but I tend to save those for special projects. Manila is the color of everyday business in my world.

Magazines, Catalogs, Newsletters, and So Forth

I have several clients who are extremely attached to old magazines or catalogs. Here's my take on what can become a real space hog. If you don't read a magazine within two months, you aren't likely to do so in the future. Let it go. Stop and think for a minute about the up-market coffee drinks you buy at Starbucks. How much pleasure do they give? They only last a few minutes, and yet we're all willing to plunk down a chunk of change for the experience, right? If you flip through a magazine on the day it arrives and enjoy the photos for about five minutes, that's enough bang for your buck. You don't have to be a good girl or boy and read every word. Is it time to stop all subscriptions or maybe a few? If so, you need to let the distributers know your relationship has come to an end when the subscription runs out. If you see a particularly interesting issue in the supermarket, buy it. By the way, I never pay for a subscription with a credit card because it usually automatically renews. I make the company send me an invoice so I can decide if I wish to continue.

Catalogs are fun, but saving them baffles me, especially when most are sent out monthly and nudge you to spend money. When the new one arrives, ditch the old. Store magazines and catalogs in a container designed to hold them rather than a generic basket. Position them to stand up so you can grab one easily. If they are in a stack, you are less likely to go through them. We're looking for a dynamic way to handle them.

If you are a member of a profession that produces trade journals (think medical professionals and lawyers), secure digital subscriptions. It's easier to store a CD than a physical copy of a magazine. I've had precious few clients who ever read these magazines. At least they represent a tax deduction.

One of my clients was an amazing interior designer. Every square inch of her garage was devoted to magazine storage because she felt her collection was a great source of inspiration. It was a great source of food for rats and other creatures, but I digress. I once asked when she had last gotten on a ladder to check a stack of magazines perched on a high shelf. She laughed and said, "Never!" I presume today she logs on to Pinterest, where you can find inspiration for home design, parties, weddings, landscaping, travel, and everything in between. When the party is over or the design project is complete, you can simply delete the board you created to support that project.

Rightsize Your Life Activity: Cut Through the Paper Debris

Go through your office, family room, and any other spot where you have magazines and catalogs. Following the above advice, slash your way fearlessly through your stash, and box up what you need to take with you to the new location. If you are honest and realize you intend to take it all and have boxes of magazines and catalogues, it's time to spend a few minutes making decisions in this home. Look at a magazine, and if you see an article you want, tear it out. It's easier to have a file folder of magazine articles you wish to read than several boxes of magazines. If you receive a catalog every month please don't take the current one with you. A fresh one will arrive at your new location if you simply include this entity in your address-change project. And if the company loses your new address, will the world come to an end? Nope. All catalogs can be found online. If it helps motivate you, set a timer and work in twenty-minute increments. Do not respond to text messages, check your e-mail, or answer the phone. Let all social media friends wait to hear about your day. Turn on music or do this in silence. Be sure you have healthy snacks and water. Make this as easy as you can. And if you really want to go crazy, post before and after shots on Instagram. "Look what I did today!" Your friends will be inspired to emulate you.

Packing Tips for the Office

Books get placed in boxes with their spines facing up. You'll have room on top to place decorative, lightweight items. Be sure you wrap every item in a lot of paper so it doesn't move around inside the box during transit. If you want to keep your collection pristine, pack books tightly enough to prevent movement. I would put paper on the top to fill in the gap and protect the small items you may have added. You don't want the box to cave if another gets placed on top of it. This is a good time to take stock of what's in your office because you may not need to pack all of it. Here are some guidelines:

- Is your home office top-heavy with family photos? Is it time to transfer some of them to albums? It's so easy to have photos on display of your children as toddlers when they just graduated from college. It may be fun for you, but they'd rather the images be current.

- Did you go crazy at a big-box store and stock up on pens, pencils, sharpies, and highlighters? These items dry up. Check that they are still viable.

- What about paper clips, scotch tape, and staples? How long have you had these items? It may be better to give some of your stash to a friend, a school, or the office at your house of worship if it isn't likely you'll use them in the next year. Space is a valuable commodity.

- Are you a big plant person? Movers will move plants over a short distance, but if you are traveling hundreds of miles or crossing state lines, it would be better to find these plants loving homes.

- Do you have office equipment you will never use again? Is some of it broken? A charity needs these items.

- What about your furniture? Is it time to refresh?

- Do you want all of the artwork on your walls to go to the new office? If you can give away or donate any of it, do so this week. If it would be better placed in a different room in the new house, be sure it's packed with items for that room.

- When you pack your equipment, be sure you tie the cords neatly so they don't turn into snakes in a box and label them. You can waste a lot of time at the other end wondering which piece of equipment a particular cord powers. If you don't have tags, just put items relating to the machine in question in a plastic bag and identify the contents on the bag. I'd use a Ziploc bag so you are sure it's sealed.

- On a related note, bag and label all the screws and other small pieces that go with your furniture no matter what room you are in. I can't tell you how many times I've had to send my assistant to a hardware store to get those supports that hold a shelf in place because the owner had no clue where they were. If the mover hasn't taped them to the back of the piece, you'll be on a hunt for something relatively unimportant, and time will be flying by.

- Finally, if you have a filing cabinet, it's a good idea to lock it and put the key in a safe place, such as your key chain or change purse.

Junk mail is an issue for many people, especially those who feel they must open each envelope and examine the contents. Here are three ways to stanch the flow of unwanted mail into your home. The trees thank you.

- Mark the envelope "return to sender" and drop it in a mailbox.
- Use the prepaid envelope provided to send back all material and include a note asking to be removed from the list.
- Call the Red Plum Mailing list at 888-241-6760 to stop delivery of flyers.
- Remember the junk clutter in your inbox and take time to unsubscribe from unwanted, unsolicited e-mails and those that simply no longer hold your interest. I find myself doing this each calendar quarter.

Office Moving-Day Box

Every move brings paperwork, and you'll want to keep it all together so you can easily reference any material related to this day. This will include the estimate from your mover, insurance policies, and so forth. This box is also a great place to keep the move file you created to catch any confirmation mail you received from organizations like the DMV and your bank. This box can also hold your checkbook and legal documents like passports should you not have a lockable filing cabinet. With that said, this box must be secured in a safe spot at your new location along with your purse. If you have the benefit of a personal car, the trunk is the obvious choice. If not, choose your spot carefully on the big day. I'm not worried about your movers. I'm thinking how easy it is for passersby to lift a box. Better to be safe than sorry, right?

If you are moving with school-age children transferring to a different school or district, you will no doubt have to keep track of some paperwork relating to that transition. I'd keep these records in this box because you don't want to have to search for them at the next location. If your school communications are all digital, be sure you keep everything in an easy-to-find, clearly marked folder on your computer.

Sacred Clutter

Over the years I have learned that the boxes for electronic equipment become sacred objects to most people, especially guys. I had a client, a doctor by profession and a computer nerd by devotion, who used the loft area in his garage to store every box that had ever entered his home containing an electronic or computer-related purchase. I was helping him prepare the home for his future wife and suggested that she and her sons might need the loft space for storage. He panicked at the very idea of tossing any of those boxes and rented a storage space for them. What can I say? Sacred clutter comes in all shapes and sizes.

If you just made a purchase, I understand wanting the original box for the period during which the initial warranty is good, and that's usually ninety days. If you are using professional movers, trust me when I tell you that they know how to pack electronic equipment safely. I kept my laptop with me when I moved. I was traveling across town and had access to my car. But if you are packing a desktop, laptop, printer, and monitor, cushioning is key. Even if you use the original box and packing materials, you want to place these items securely in larger moving boxes, allowing no movement inside. Here are some basic steps to help secure these expensive and vital components of modern life:

- Check the instruction manual that came with the item. It probably has moving tips and instructions. If you no longer have that or can't find it, go online to the company website and see if you can download a copy. If all else fails, talk to a customer service representative and express your concerns.

- If your equipment has detachable parts, pack them separately. If liquid is involved, like toner or ink, pack it in plastic and keep all parts together in one box.

- A box store will sell you a special box for any large, delicate equipment. You may also be able to get the original box from the manufacturer. Put out a call on Craigslist.org or social media sites if you have time. A friend may have the right box in his sacred clutter stash and let you borrow it.

- If, like me, you will be lost if cables are pulled, be sure to use colored labels, tape, or some other means of identification so that you can reconnect everything at the other end. If you have a smart phone, you can also take a photo or make a video.

- Use twist ties on cables, cords, and wires so you don't have electronic spaghetti at the other end. Keep all items in a Ziploc bag labeled for the piece of equipment they serve.

- Your best china, valuable collectibles, and electronic equipment need an extra amount of paper on the bottom of the box. Go ahead and be indulgent. Better safe than sorry. If you put more than one piece of equipment in a box, be sure you pad between items and fill in all gaps. Needless to say, you need to layer heaviest on the bottom to lightest on the top. When you shake the box, there should be no movement. If you are using some other type of packing material, like bubble wrap or popcorn, be sure it's antistatic.

- These boxes must be labeled "Fragile: Do Not Stack," and please indicate the top of the box. As with all boxes, note the contents and room destination.
- Seal with packing tape.

I can hear some of you now asking why I suggest you discard the original box and packing material if you will need them when you move. I think there are many valuable commodities in life, and my list includes time, money, food, and space. Yes, I consider space sacred. If you have a loft in your garage and you feel more secure holding on to boxes, by all means do so. For the rest of us, those empty boxes will hog the space and clog the energy under the bed or in the back of a closet or wherever you stash them. In using a space, weigh the time you will be in the home against the cost of a few boxes on moving day. The choice is yours. If you decide to keep everything, do me one favor: as equipment is sold, tossed, given away, or donated, please send it off in the original box. And don't forget to include the warranties and instruction manuals.

Planning for the Next Home Office

No matter the size of your next workspace, plan for how you will do the business of life in your new home. Try to place your desk so that your back is against the wall and you are seated looking out into the room and not in the doorway. These are traditional Feng Shui principles, which I realize may not interest you; however, correct placement will make you feel more powerful. As my friend Ariel Joseph Towne, the Feng Shui Guy, asks, Where does the godfather sit in a restaurant? Is his back to the room, or is he in a commanding position in the back of the restaurant where he can easily survey the space? Interestingly enough, you'll notice corporate heads and military officers naturally make the same choice. I want you to feel empowered.

Be sure the equipment that serves you is close at hand. If you constantly have to walk across the room to the printer or any other tool you use regularly, you are wasting time. Keep plants and photos under control. Why not have photos on a computer program that rotates them randomly? Instead of looking at the same faces, you'll be constantly surprised. If you love plants, as I do, either have the traditional money tree plant in this room for luck, or if you have a lot of plants, get a stand for them near a window.

If your office will double as a guest room or other type of room, be sure the space is clearly divided. Rugs and wall art help define a space. I had a client who had to have his desk in his living room, but he didn't want his friends looking at his work when they came over to watch a game. We moved the rug and the furniture so that

MYTH OF THE BLACK THUMB

Not only are plants beautiful, but they clean and purify the air. Many of my clients tell me they have a black thumb. Too many times to count, they have spent good money on beautiful plants, only to bring them home and watch them wither and die. I can almost always pinpoint the culprit, and it's never a black thumb. You need to match the plant to the conditions in the room. Rather than making an emotion-based decision, ask for help at a nursery. Plants also often die because people forget to water them. Set an alarm on your smart phone or computer, or tie watering to an external reminder. When I hear the theme music for *60 Minutes* start on Sunday night, I know it's time to give all my plants a drink. If you will not make a plan to water your plants, don't bring them home. Consider silk plants.

his desk was behind the couch and off the rug. This visually isolated the desk, and no one ever invaded his work privacy again.

If the office serves periodically as a guest room, be sure you provide some closet space for your guests, but don't give them a king-size bed that leaves you working at a tiny desk in the corner. You'd be surprised how many people sacrifice day-to-day comfort in order to honor the guests who stay maybe two weeks per year. A bookcase placed in the closet can become the office-supply storage area for the room.

Week's Summary

- ❏ Defang your paper phobia by uncovering the fear behind it.
- ❏ Try meditation.
- ❏ Investigate the three main reasons people avoid making decisions about paper.
- ❏ Sort paper piles; toss, shred, or recycle as needed.
- ❏ Archive old tax records and projects.
- ❏ Set up files to catch current material.
- ❏ Sort through reading matter like magazines, catalogs, newsletters, and so forth.
- ❏ Clean out the existing filing cabinet.
- ❏ Gather all warranties and instructions, and sort for ease of retrieval.
- ❏ Set up a simple office file system.
- ❏ Set up action files.
- ❏ Consider purchasing basic office supplies.
- ❏ Cull through small office supplies and decorative items.
- ❏ Consider the set up of the next office.
- ❏ Read packing tips.

A Closing Thought

For most of you this will be one of the toughest weeks leading up to your downsize and move. Paper is difficult for many to process. It also tells the story of your life in many ways. As we sort and purge, we confront our former interests, the money we have spent on education or home repairs, and even our earnings for a particular year, all of which can send us down an emotional road. If you love music, this is the week to fill your home with it as you slog through the debris of unmade decisions called paper piles. And if, like me, you love solitude, reward yourself with a few extra minutes of meditation. Congratulations on completing a really tough series of assignments.

FAMILY TIES

I take to the open road, healthy, free,
the world before me.
—WALT WHITMAN

RIGHT ABOUT NOW YOU'RE PROBABLY SO SICK OF YOUR
possessions that making decisions about what stays and what goes
is getting pretty easy. I have a word of caution. Continue to do your
self-care rituals and keep as balanced a schedule as you can. As moving day draws near you can get what I call "the Fever." Suddenly very
little is sacred, and you want to pitch most of what you own. I don't
want you to experience any regrets in the new home.

The Crash Pad: Packing Living Areas

Pity the poor family room with multiple users. People flounce in,
make a mess, and exit without a thought about the others who will
follow. The newspaper is separated into sections, and each flies all
over the room, landing ultimately in scattered heaps of newsprint.

SELF-CARE TIP FOR THE WEEK

THIS WEEK MY self-care tip revisits an idea I presented in week three: get out into nature. Nature has a way of calming us like nothing else. The family room won't be the bear the office was; nor will it be as emotional as your children's rooms. Go crazy and visit the local botanical garden or the zoo. Jump on a swing, and swing high as if no one can see you. Feed peanuts to the elephants (if it's allowed). Surely your city has a park. Even Manhattan boasts Central Park! Sit on a bench and read a chapter in that book you've wanted to start. Don't make it a family outing; just call your best buddy or go alone. Forget the move for a few hours and breathe. The work you do when you return will be easier and go much faster. On the off chance that your move is taking place in the middle of the coldest winter on record and you simply can't get out into nature, try eating these foods that are great for the liver (in traditional Chinese medicine the organ most affected by strong emotions): avocados, dandelion greens, soy foods, onions, nuts, and seeds. If you are open to it, this might be the perfect time for a healing treatment. You can choose from the worlds of acupuncture, chiropractic, and massage. It sounds silly but you will thank me later when you feel refreshed, restored, and renewed. Try to find a practitioner whose work you know rather than just searching your local phone book or Google. Not all practitioners are equally gifted. As we embark on week six, you deserve the best.

Unfinished food sits on plates while drinking glasses are stained with the residue of unidentifiable liquids. A DVD either remains in the machine or was popped into the closest container when a new one was inserted. The same haphazard fate meets the CDs. If young children are in the house, stuffed animals are everywhere. Board games are falling apart, and pieces from different games are jumbled together. Pillows and throws designed to keep you comfy and warm are scattered all over the floor like rumpled old clothes. Fido and Fifi use the space with the same nonchalance. In fact, they have turned those pillows and throws into makeshift beds. Cat and dog toys litter the landscape. In most homes, patient parents dutifully restore order, right? We're going to kiss this behavior good-bye in the new home. Are you with me? But the first thing we have to do is sort through the debris to see what's there, what needs to go, what's making the journey, and what you can donate. As we move from room to room, you realize the truth of what I told you at the start: organizing is organizing; only the material in your hands changes. This week is all about pleasure-inducing items. Let's get started.

Speed Eliminations to the Rescue

Let's do a few of these speed eliminations in quick succession, shall we? Each time we will be on the lookout for only one type of item. This kind of laser focus will help you move quickly and begin to relieve any congestion in the room.

- Round 1—orphaned items: Set your kitchen timer or the alarm on your cell phone for ten minutes and make it your business to gather all the orphaned items in the room. I bet there are dishes or glasses that have to go to the kitchen. If you have very young children, some toys that belong in their rooms may have been left here. Has anyone left jackets and sweaters that belong in the entry closet or some other spot? You get the idea. Gather items in categories near the room's entrance. When your ten minutes is up, take each category in turn to the place it belongs, unless of course you know it's not making the move with you. You can start a donation box.

- Round 2—paper: This time out you want to be on the hunt for paper. Gather magazines, newspapers, mail, homework, and so forth. Again, make neat, separated piles near the entry. Mail has a designated spot now that you've organized your office area. Homework should be kept wherever your child does it. Toss magazines older than two months and newspapers older than two days. Clip and file any articles you feel you need after the alarm sounds. You can experience the benefits of the work you did last week.

- Round 3—toys: This time, you may need a twenty-minute work session. I want you to examine all the toys in this room. Have your children outgrown some? Has your family not enjoyed some of the board games in months? Gather toys in related categories (e.g., board games, stuffed animals). When the alarm sounds, examine each item, one category at a time. If your children are no longer toddlers, you will have to consult with them. Place all the toys you'd like to toss or donate in one area. Explain to children that you need to make room for new items, and if the items are still in decent condition, you'd like to give them to a charity so a less fortunate child can enjoy them. If these items are no longer needed but your children are having emotional problems with the impending move, box up the items but don't seal the box. Set it in another room or the garage. See what, if anything, is missed.

- Round 4—what's left: Our final work session today is to take stock of the items now remaining in this room. Is all the furniture going with you, or should some of it be donated? Will you use what you take in the new family room or somewhere else? Be sure you know before moving day so you can direct the movers. Examine furniture and items like pillows and throws.

This is more than enough work for one day. I'm going to bet the rest of the family will be flabbergasted when they see the family room. Even though it isn't organized yet, it has less in it, and the feel of the room will be lighter and more inviting.

Eat your Wheaties!

The Book Collector's Dilemma

Today you will be removing books that are ready for a new home. Let me share a personal anecdote that may help you understand just how delicious it can be to share books. My first profession was acting. I had a large collection of plays, and I held on to them when I switched to organizing and writing. I dedicated a separate bookcase to my treasures. One day I realized that these old friends now sat idle, like a monument to a part of my life that was over. They belonged in the hands of young actors. They needed to be enjoyed and cherished. I boxed them up and donated them to a high school for the performing arts. I've never felt better about any decision I've made to give something away.

A client of mine was preparing to retire from the law. He had practiced and been a judge. He was a borderline hoarder and had held on to all the books from his days in law school. It took a bit of effort to find a school that wanted forty-year-old textbooks, but ultimately they went off to become part of a rich archival treasure trove of material one school kept for its students. This was a much better fate for them than gathering dust in my client's home office.

I suggest a speed elimination to start so that you don't get too involved with any particular volume. This isn't the day to revisit that novel you loved, the biography that inspired you, or the atlas that fires your wanderlust. To begin, set your timer for ten or twenty minutes (depending on the size of your collection) and scan your books for those ready to give enjoyment to some other person or group. Think outside the box. Consider donating to convalescent homes, libraries, secondhand bookshops (I presume there's at least one left somewhere in America!), hospitals, schools, or clubs. As you pull them off the shelves keep them in categories. This will save time in the event categories go to separate entities rather than to one new owner.

It is also possible to find new homes for your books online at sites where you can buy, sell, trade, or collect credits. Remember that you aren't going to get a huge amount for your books, so consider whether you can spare the time to list your treasures. What happens, for example, if you end up with several boxes of books waiting for new homes? You may want to donate these items and then use the websites for future purchases. I'm trying to safeguard your time as we move ever closer to moving day.

As you make your distribution, think ahead to next April 15 and how delighted you'll be to have all these donation receipts for your taxes. A tax deduction may mean more to you than the cash or credit you might earn. If you find the right new home for your books (or toys, music, etc.) but can't get a receipt, you may be content to know that these items are once again being cherished. Money and tax credits aren't the only worthwhile rewards.

The Electronic Festival: What to Do with Media Collections

Music and movies pose a problem for the collector. If you are under thirty, you live in an all-digital world and can't imagine what the fuss is about. The rest of us have myriad records, cassette tapes, CDs, and DVDs cluttering up the environment. Let's talk about each in turn and examine an overarching principle that will keep your media world under control. As technology changes means of enjoying and organizing media will no doubt emerge after this book is published. If you aren't a "techie," stay connected to a teenager who knows the latest and the greatest.

Records were out of fashion for a long time, but now the word on the street is that they produce the best sound. If your record collection is sacred to you, I understand. Do you currently have a record player? If you do, create a spot in your next family room near where the player is set up so you can easily enjoy your collection. The shelves of a deep bookcase or display unit work nicely. You can get shelving at IKEA or storage cubes at The Container Store or google something like "vinyl record storage and display" for specialty stores. It depends on how much you treasure the collection, how often you enjoy it, and how much you can comfortably spend.

If your collection is sentimental at this point and not going to be enjoyed, do invest in special storage boxes, designed specifically to hold vinyl records, from The Container Store or any big-box store. If you are going to store these in the back of a closet, don't stack them, and don't keep them in a place like the attic or garage, where the temperature isn't controlled, as extremes and humidity can cause damage. You may want to play these in the future or keep them as an investment. No one will enjoy the vinyl if the record is warped. Mark these boxes clearly as "Fragile: Do Not Stack" in big, bold letters. Before you pack your treasures away, consider having your favorite album cover framed for display in the new family room. If there's a photo of you from the era when you enjoyed this music, have that photo framed as well for display close by. It's a sweet touch when a room helps tell your story without your ever having to utter a single word.

As a professional organizer who has trucked in and out of homes for twenty-five years, I have noticed that in general men are far more particular than women about their media collections. We women seem content to divide our music and movies by type; men will take the time to alphabetize by artist. If you have that kind of patience and time, I bow down before you. I don't. I like to look at a collection and divide it by type. Let's say your music tastes run something like this:

- Broadway
- Country

- Funk
- Jazz
- Rap

You notice I did alphabetize the categories! I would divide and sort or store my records in this fashion. My media collection might be done along these lines:

- Biography
- Children
- Comedies
- Documentaries
- Dramas

Some of my clients must have their CDs in their original jewel cases. They like to reference the liner notes. If that's you, then by all means divide your collection in a way that makes sense to you and then pop your treasures into a media cabinet or unit designed to hold them. Check out the selections at a store like Best Buy for ideas. You can get a unit that looks like a traditional bookcase or buy a metal tower. Your purchase will be dictated by the number of CDs and DVDs you have. Needless to say, they will soon go the way of the dinosaur and you may need a cabinet designed specifically for Blu-ray.

Many of my clients join me in placing those wonderful CDs and DVDs into binders. You can store the original packaging if you want to sell or trade the original one day. Then you divide your collection as above and slip the disc into a special storage sheet that pops into a standard binder. You can use utilitarian ones from a big-box store like Staples or go all-out and purchase fancy leather binders monogrammed for your family. The choice is yours. I like Levengers and Exposures for fine leather binders.

Over the past few years, my small collection has grown as I now purchase all my entertainment on iTunes. I'm a Mac person and store everything on the Cloud, where I can easily access it with any Apple device. It doesn't bother me that I can't touch the product, but I remember that joy from childhood, so I have a foot in both camps. Here's the bottom line: the things you own and the ways you enjoy them are your business. Please don't tell anyone else that his or her collection is old-fashioned. There are two key factors: Do you enjoy what you collect, and can you find what you own? If you answer yes to both questions, you're good to go.

I'm going to close this section with a word about cassettes and VHS tapes. I bet you don't have a cassette player, do you? Technology gets outmoded, and we know that tapes are not coming back. This may be an emotional culling for many of you because your collection will be fraught with memories. If you have cassettes with the voices of deceased loved ones or music by some artist whose work is no longer available (or you don't want to pay twice for the same entertainment), put those treasures in a box to store in the back of a closet. For family videotapes, consider a VHS-to-DVD converter. Remember that you can transfer old media to disc and enjoy it again; that's not always a cheap proposition, however, so make those choices wisely. And yes, this can wait until after your move.

Before we leave this area, I'm certain that this room has equipment that is no longer used. You probably set it aside because it wasn't cheap and you wanted it for backup or some other reason that seemed logical. Why not assess all the equipment you have and keep only what you use? TVs and all the players that make individual types of media accessible have come down in price. You can get a decent thirty-two-inch TV for $200 at a big-box store. Why keep monitors, DVD players, and old cassette players around, robbing you of space when you could send them on to a new home? Once again, remember that Goodwill does repair electronic items. You can devote the space you gain to a hobby in the next family room. Never considered that, did you?

Outlets for the Stuff in Our Lives

You can trade or sell your books, furniture, and other collectibles on many sites, I'm sure, but I'm going to play it safe and share with you the obvious choices. It is important to deal with well-established businesses that have been around long enough to earn our trust. I'm including a few great sites for donations here as well. You may find that selling takes more time than you can dedicate to the process if you only have a few weeks left. If you are downsizing for a future move, on the other hand, you might make enough to pay for the mover—or at the very least for meals and tips on the big day!

- Amazon's textbook trade-in program: This is a great way to reduce the expense of textbooks. It also teaches your child to be careful with his or her possessions because you earn more for books in good condition. Amazon makes it possible to ship your approved texts for free, and once they sell, you get an Amazon gift card.

- Amazon.com direct sales: You can investigate the details for both programs at Amazon.com. This second option effectively makes you an instant merchant who can sell any number of products, not just books.

- PaperBackSwap.com: This site deals with all types of books (e.g., fiction, nonfiction, children's books, textbooks). You can choose a few from your collection and do a comparison to see which site offers you the best deal. PaperBackSwap.com has a social media aspect and likes members to interact. Joining is free, and if you are an avid reader moving to a new area, this site may open the door to new friends as a bonus.

- Discovery Shops. These wonderful stores are part of the American Cancer Society, so your donations generate a tax receipt, and you have the satisfaction of knowing you are supporting a good cause. I gave furniture none of my friends wanted to my local store when it became clear that used furniture was a big pain in the neck to sell for little profit. My local Discovery Shop, like most, picked up large pieces of furniture in good condition at no charge. These shops take gently used items in all categories except major appliances, mattresses, and intimate apparel.

- Goodwill.com. This great organization has centers around the United States. I appreciate most that its outlets can repair broken items. That printer, washer, or TV you haven't used in six months will be refurbished, get a new home, and make a profit for this wonderful group.

- Craigslist.org: You can sell just about anything here, and categories represent the items you have to offer. This is a great way to sell items you need someone local to pick up. Although I have no doubt you will connect with an honest person, allow me to give you a word of caution: Don't give out any personal information to the buyer. He or she doesn't need to know you are moving or that you live alone and have a seven-pound guard dog named Killer. Ask a friend to be present if the item is too big for you to take to a local coffee shop for the exchange and borrow a friend's pit bull. He's probably named Tiny or Muffin, but during the meeting call him Killer. Better safe than sorry.

- eBay.com: It is fair to say that you can buy or sell just about anything on this site. Some people devote a great deal of time to selling, and they are your competition if you are new to auction sales. By that I mean they have the sales lingo down and know how to work the system to get the best deal. You may not be interested in learning the ins and outs of eBay. You may have zero aptitude at writing great copy. You need to consider the value of what you have to sell, the time you have to devote, and how interested you are in the process. Selling a few items may launch you into a permanent way to make some money on the side. It may also send you into the arms of my next choice.

- GotJunk.com: At the end of your eight weeks, if you find your-self with a lot of items you don't want to schlep to the new lo-cation, you might need GotJunk.com. A friend of mine found herself in this position a few years ago. She had to leave her apartment by a set date and fell behind in her preparations. She hired GotJunk.com to come in and remove what was left because the building management would have charged a great deal more. GotJunk.com seeks to recycle, donate, or dispose of responsibly whatever items you present. It has kept 1.5 billion pounds of junk out of landfills since its start in 1989. You just have to get past the idea that your stuff is now "junk." It isn't. That's just a catchy word for a business that helps a lot of folks!

- Local charity of your choice: You certainly have the opportunity to help an organization whose work you admire. I particularly like Goodwill because it can fix broken items and then sell them.

- Local women's shelters: These may take and sell items to help clients who are starting over; in some cases, they use the items to furnish a home for a family.

- Consignment stores: You can make a little money on your old furniture and collectibles and start a fund for fresh purchases.

- Half.com: This is a site like Amazon but bases its fee on the price of your item.

- Threadflip.com: This is a wonderful site if you have vintage or designer clothing to off-load. It takes a percentage.

- Freecycle.org: You list items you are giving away, and it's just that easy.

Here are some tips for dealing with specific types of items:

- Cellphones can be given to your local women's shelter or to CellPhones for Soldiers, located in Texas with a few regional drop-off centers. Check online to see if there's one in your neighborhood. You can also just mail in a gently used phone and make it possible for a soldier to phone home. There are other ways but I personally love these two because they directly help those in need. Be sure you wipe the phone clean of your personal data!

- Computers are filled with toxic chemicals so you don't want to toss them into a landfill. Every community has a special drop-off center for discarded technology-related items, including all batteries used in the home and light bulbs. It takes a bit of effort to dispose of these items correctly, but it's worth it because you're saving the earth for future generations. Give your trash company a call for directions in your community. IKEA will now recycle batteries, as will Whole Foods. The latter also accepts paper and light bulbs. I would call your local store for particulars as they may vary from location to location. Recycle batteries by mail through BatteryRecycling.com.

- If you are off-loading a computer, monitor, or printer that still works, give your local school district a call. A school might be able to make good use of your castoffs.

- Finally, take old computer equipment to one of these three great charities: The National Christina Foundation, the World Computer Exchange, and Computers with Causes. Computers with Causes helps families in need get a home computer, and the National Christina Foundation will match your donated hardware to nonprofits in need. As the name suggests, the World Computer Exchange helps those in need around the world get electronic equipment.

As with your cellphones, please be sure to wipe your hard drive clean of all your personal data before you make any type of donation. If you don't know how to do this, check your instruction manual if you still have it. You can also call the manufacturer or find a teenager who knows about electronics. Instead of collecting dust and taking up space, these items can help others in communities around the globe get connected. Whether or not you get a tax credit is immaterial. You've helped someone out. You can also contact Call2Recycle.com.

If you are selling an item, first do a little market research. If the price is right, you'll make a quick sale and be done. Great photos also move items on websites like eBay. And just as you would for a yard sale, be sure to handle any repairs before you advertise. Obviously you want to set yourself up to win, but you'd be surprised how many folks defeat themselves because they secretly don't want to let an item go. You see this phenomenon with homes that have fantasy price tags rather than ones based on property values in the neighborhood.

Here are some creative resources for donating your books:

- OperationPaperback.org: This site connects you with troops overseas who might enjoy your books. Be mindful that you pay for shipping.
- AccessBooks.net: Whenever there's a disaster, we immediately think of people needing food, shelter, and water. But if you are going to be in a shelter for an extended period, you might want to read a book. And that's where AccessBooks.com helps out. You can put your books into a backpack if you have one and even add a note of encouragement for the recipient.

These resources will help you find a home for your old friends that you couldn't feel better about.

Ye Old Yard Sale

For those of you who love to attend and organize yard sales, these paragraphs are immaterial. You have a passion and knack for this type of sale. For those who shy away from yard sales, I have tucked this material toward the end because it's really a last resort for you. Having been dragged to every antique show and yard sale on the eastern seaboard by my mother when I was a child, I am in this boat with you. A successful yard sale depends on three key elements: good-quality items priced to sell, a great location (good weather doesn't hurt), and a well-organized plan. See? You don't have to love them to know how to host them!

If your move is in the distant future, you have the luxury of time. If your move is on the horizon, you need to weigh the benefits. Here are some questions to ask:

- Some communities require a permit to host a yard sale, so get your legal ducks in a row. This action will of course put your sale on the government's radar, and you may have to pay tax on your earnings.

- What day did you have in mind? Early Saturday morning is great because you can call Sunday as your backup day in the event of rain.

- Do you have items that sell well at yard sales? Popular items include tools, toys, sporting equipment, kitchen appliances, and general household items.

- If everything gets sold, will you make enough to offset the time and energy holding a yard sale requires?

- Do you have friends or neighbors who will help share the workload? Setting up, dealing with the public, and taking down your displays is exhausting work.

- Do large pieces of furniture need to be carried outside? Do you have strong individuals who can handle the task?

- Folding tables and chairs, along with portable racks for clothing items, are key. Are they available? Well-presented merchandise has a better chance of selling than items tossed into a careless heap.

- How will you get the word out? You can paste flyers all over the neighborhood to announce the sale, mention it on social media, announce it at work if you have a bulletin board (electronic or physical) where such announcements are allowed, and place an ad in the *PennySaver*. You'll also want to call, text, or e-mail your family and friends so that they can share the sale date with their communities. Many yard sale devotees check Craigslist. org and the local paper. The former is free, but the latter charges a modest fee to list your sale in its classifieds. Be sure you're included in the online version. This is an important sale, so go all-out to make it a success.

- Who in your group is good at designing flyers? And who will post them, then take them down after the sale? You don't want to create hard feelings in your community before you leave. Posted signs initially direct your neighbors to your sale; once it's over, those same signs turn into trash that no one wants you to leave behind.

If you have answers or positive responses to these questions, then I'd say it's time to host a yard sale in two weeks. If you hold it just before your move, you will have that much less to pack! Be sure you arrange for transfer to a charity any items that do not sell. You may wish to take a look around your garage, attic, or basement. I've tucked those areas into week eight because they are not common to everyone, but you would be wise to take a quick look for sellable items. Now that you've agreed to have a yard sale, I have a few final words of wisdom.

- When you have selected your items, be sure they are in tip-top shape. Put any needed laundering, mending, or polishing on your to-do list for next week.

- Sort your items into categories. On the big day, you don't want *War and Peace* holding your blouses in place. You catch my drift. I told you there was power in categories at the outset, didn't I?

- Purchase tags at a local office-supply store and have everything clearly priced. Yard sales attract hagglers. Know in advance how low you are willing to go.

- Have a prominent sign announcing that a percentage of the sale's proceeds will go to your favorite charity (and name it on the sign). People may be inclined to spend more and haggle less if they know you are doing good in the process of transferring the clutter from your home to theirs!

- Unless it's a woman in labor, no one should be allowed into your home to use your bathroom or phone or anything else. Be sure you know where the nearest public bathroom is located.

- You'll want a responsible adult to man the cashbox, which should contain $50 in singles so you can make change. If you have a smart phone, you can sign up for free at Square.com and accept credit cards. But this would be for items over a selected amount because you're going to lose a small percentage in the transaction. Cash is king.

- If you don't have a dog, borrow a friend's. People don't need to see the pup; they just need to hear him bark if they go too near the house. An ounce of prevention is worth a pound of cure.

- Invite an enterprising child in your family or on your street to sell lemonade if it's a hot day.

- Get an extra box of sturdy trash bags at the grocery store and a few sturdy boxes from the local liquor store and be ready to pack your treasures up and send them off in style.

- When the sale is over, take in everything you brought out for the sale. You don't want your neighbors to be delighted you're getting out of Dodge. And, once again, don't forget to take down those flyers you distributed. You want the entire neighborhood to remember you fondly!

Do you have confirmation that your utilities are going to be turned on at the new location when you move? Will they be shut off in your current residence? Have you gathered in a special place the documents you may need on moving day, like the estimate from the mover or the rental agreement for the truck? Some of your moving-day documents have no doubt come to you via e-mail. Be sure you collect it all in one folder on your computer. You want to avoid the refrain "I know I have it here somewhere!" At the beginning of this journey I asked you to spend time getting these paper ducks in a row. The big day is on the horizon, and now is the time to be absolutely certain that nothing has been left to chance.

Planning for the Next Family Room

It's time to decide the fate of the furniture in this room and to cull through your collections. Remember that you are making room for the books, music, and movies you and your family will enjoy in the next home. I earlier noted the casual way this room is treated. In the next family room, you are going to be streamlined, categorized, and organized. The room is going to function more efficiently, whether it's bigger or smaller. A key factor will be in the execution of something I call "completion" and the assignment of chores. I think these two life-enhancing concepts ought to be universally embraced, and the family room is an ideal place to practice.

Completion refers to moving consciously through your day and being certain to finish any action you start. What do I mean? If you are home now, get up and walk around. Are all the cupboards closed? Are any drawers left open? Do tasks like tossing the trash begin and then end with the garbage bag by the door? Or perhaps the trash is out, but now there's no bag in the container. Did the clothes you picked up at the dry cleaner last week stay on the chair in your bedroom? When we are distracted, preoccupied, or depressed, this type of thing can happen. But it can easily become a habit, and that's not a good thing. Aside from the fact you can bonk your head on an open cabinet door or trip on the trash or find that Fido has opened it and spread its contents over the floor, there is a metaphor here. If you are not completing simple actions in the home or your office, I guarantee you aren't completing actions in your life. Does your to-do list never diminish? There's a sign. Do you fail to follow through on promises to friends and family? There's another. The examples are limitless.

In this room you will see examples of your generosity to your children. Too many toys, media, and electronic gadgets litter the landscape. Generosity of the material kind is very often a balm for the guilt we feel for working long hours or not making time to play. Sometimes a concept is a greater gift than anything you can put in a box. If your children grow up with completion as an ingrained habit, they will have easier lives. When everything that serves us returns to a designated spot, the environment stays tidy, and many minutes are saved. How many times have you wanted to watch a particular movie or listen to a piece of music only to find the disc has been put away in a random jewel case? This is a waste of time, and if it happens frequently, like the classic hunt for keys, glasses, or the remote, you can see how much of your life is wasted on trivial pursuits. Pennies make dollars, and minutes make hours. And those hours make up a life.

Many parents regard chores as tasks that rob a child of freedom. After all, they tell me, you are only young once. I agree. But if you leave for college at eighteen with no clue how to manage a household, you are going to be in a pickle. Today you are asked to clean up your room. Tomorrow you'll be given homework assignments. The next day you'll be running your own home. It's a continuum, with the nature of the responsibilities evolving as you mature, and completion is the key. When John F. Kennedy Jr. went to college, he shared a home with two or three others, including correspondent Christiane Amanpour. In an interview after his tragic death, she said they all took turns cleaning, including the bathroom. If the scion of a large fortune can clean the house toilet while at college, your child can do chores and follow his example.

Finally, as you design the new family room and consider what you need to part with or repurchase, think about the activities you want to perform in this room. Does someone in the family need a space for a hobby or crafts? Will this room accommodate those interests? If yes, what do you need to make the activity work? Inexpensive bookcases can hold office, craft, or hobby supplies. If a lack of space has denied you the pleasure of a pastime, see if you can incorporate that activity into the next family room. And as we close out this week, here are a few ideas for chores or completion actions:

- If you bring something into this room, you need to return it to its designated home. Glasses and plates, for example, go back to the kitchen.

- If you use something in this room, when you are finished, return it to its original location so that someone else can find and use the item.

- Dogs can't pick up after themselves (OK, some can, but that's another story!), so a nice chore for a child is to return all of Fido's toys to his designated basket in this room at the end of the evening.

- Magazines and newspapers should be tossed or returned to the designated magazine and newspaper holders.

- Papers and mail should migrate to the office area or the desk in this room if the family business is handled here; homework should return to where each child studies.

- All blankets should be refolded at the end of the evening.

- Fluff the pillows so the room will feel more welcoming the next day.

I have a client who has been a guest at a royal residence in Europe. Family members wear an electronic device that lets the staff know when they have left a room. The staff scurries in and tidies up, making the room fresh and welcoming each time the royal enters. You too can live the lifestyle of the rich and famous—through completion and chores. I know it's a stretch, but it was worth a shot, wasn't it?

Moving-Day Box

I can't imagine you need one unless this is where Fido and Fifi have their special beds, blankets, and toys. They will feel so welcome if these items appear the second the truck rolls out of the driveway.

Week's Summary

- ❑ Go out into nature.
- ❑ Do a speed elimination in the family room.
- ❑ Cull your book collection.
- ❑ Consider creative sources for media donations.
- ❑ Consider ideas for (nondigital) media collections.
- ❑ Investigate popular outlets for cast-off stuff.
- ❑ Hold a yard sale.
- ❑ Plan for the next family room.
- ❑ Consider the concept of completion and the importance of chores.

A Closing Thought

For people like me, this week is an easy one because I don't have a large collection of electronics or media. For the average American family, this week is very tough because off-loading some of these items serves as a reminder of money ill spent. Take heart. We all are at fault when it comes to wasting money—we simply squander it on different things. As you culled your CDs, did you find a piece of music you love and had forgotten you own? Take a bath, turn on that music, and light a candle. If you have small children, ask your partner or best friend for an hour of private time. If you have never investigated the world of aromatherapy, you have a treat in your future. Aroma can have a potent effect on our psyche. Citrus revives us, sandalwood is meditative, lavender relaxes us, and musk is romantic. Add something to your bath, and enjoy the music. It has powers to sooth the savage beast as well as those who are getting ready to move. I swear.

CHILDREN'S ROOMS

Do not encumber your mind with
useless thoughts.
What good does it do to
brood on the past
or anticipate the future?
Remain in the simplicity of
the present moment.

—Dilgo Khyentse Rinpoche

Child's Play

EVERY PARENT WILL HAVE A DIFFERENT JOURNEY THIS WEEK, depending on the number and ages of children in the home and how attached they are to their stuff. You won't be shocked to learn that their attachment or lack thereof reflects an unconscious desire either to emulate or rebel against you. I have worked with a lot of teenagers who tell me the shocking state of their room is a way to drive a neat parent out of his or her mind. Keep in mind that a messy room is a fairly benign form of rebellion. My only request of the teens I work with is that no food ever be left in the room. You don't want to provide a meal for the creepy crawlies in the neighborhood.

An organized, tidy, and clean friend of mine was stepmother to a young man who gave her a run for her money. The minute her stepson became a teenager and his hormones shifted, he wanted to live in a pigsty. They fought tooth and nail. When he went off to college, she felt there was no hope for him. As luck would have it, he had learned basic cooking, sewing, and laundry skills from his stepmother. He became the go-to guy in his dorm. The young man who created a pigsty at home turned into Nate Berkus when he went off to college. Take heart if you're in the middle of such a struggle. Miracles happen.

The week ahead includes a task common to all humans, whether they have children or not: whittling down memorabilia. Look at it all with an eye to where and how you will store it in the next living situation and whether you still need to hold on to all these mementos. Times change, and so do our attachments and our emotional needs. We'll also look at other popular aspects of small-space living: dorm life (instructions are adaptable for your high school grad who plans to share a first apartment with others) and retirement. I could say that many stages of life remind us that we do not in fact need all of our stuff.

Practice Makes Perfect:
Packing the Children's Rooms

You have already dealt with your bedroom, and the process here is pretty much the same, except you probably don't have toys in your room. Getting organized is a skill and nothing more; it isn't a magic act. You learn the basics, and you practice. This week you have a wonderful opportunity to teach your children a skill that will serve

SELF-CARE TIP
FOR THE WEEK

IN TODAY'S WORLD, understanding how to take care of yourself and re-lieve stress is key to survival. Why not pick one of the self-care tips you worked on in previous chapters and share it with your child? It's never too early to learn that some actions heal, and others wear you down. It's equally a great time to learn that organizing has some fun aspects.

them to the end of their lives. The skill of getting and staying orga-nized is the gift that keeps on giving.

I've said this once, but it bears repeating here: never, ever make decisions for other family members without permission unless they are under age five and not able to grasp the task and its consequences. We all feel violated when our stuff gets tossed or goes missing. I've seen spouses come home from work, sense that something of theirs has been tossed, and stop by the trash can on the way into the house! Teaching by example the power of decision-making and organizing skills will be an enormous gift to your children. Remember that the most powerful way to teach these lessons is to demonstrate them rather than just delivering a lecture on the importance of being orga-nized. I worked with a special couple once who were polar opposites. She saved nothing that wasn't key to her current life and survival, whereas he was incredibly sentimental about everything. She wanted me to assist him in learning the value of eliminating what he no longer needed, used, or wanted. I suggested she work with me before I started on her husband's area of the bedroom. She was fearless, speedy, and inspiring. Here was a minimalist willing to pare down and be realistic about what she needed. He was inspired. You can do the same for your spouse and children.

Allow children to decorate their boxes in unique ways with original drawings, stickers, or colored labels. Their boxes will be easy for the movers to spot and take to their rooms without having to ask the question that will wear you out on moving day: "Where does this go?"

The Toy Tower

Let's begin the process of clearing out a child's room with a speed elimination. Make it a game if your child is working with you. Set your timer for ten minutes. You're on the hunt for toys of all descriptions that have been outgrown or have simply fallen out of favor. When the timer sounds, examine your stash.

The next step is to sort toys by category so that you and your child can see how many stuffed animals, board games, Legos, or Barbies actually occupy this room. Once you have your categories, you'll want to move from one to the next, deciding which toys to keep, which are ready for retirement in the trash bin, and which can have a fresh start with a new child. After you whittle down the categories, you need to make one more decision: With the move on the horizon, how much can you pack up now? Board games and stuffed animals, like books, are fairly indestructible and can be popped into boxes. You might want to secure game pieces in small Ziploc bags and put a large rubber band around any worn boxes. You can purchase board game replacement boxes at The Container Store. I would also put small toys with pieces in plastic Ziploc bags. Legos can spread like a fungus, and you don't want that drama on unpack day! (If your child has a large Lego collection, you may want to purchase some storage bins with lids just for the pieces.) The bottom line is that the move is a week away, and there is no reason any child needs the usual assortment of toys at his disposal. At this point only treasured items need to be accessible.

It's important to get the trash out of the house immediately so your child can't change his mind. Out of sight, out of mind is the rule. I'd get donated items into boxes or bags and put them outside the front door or in your car or make an appointment for a pickup by your favorite charity.

I have a word of caution. If you have items earmarked for friends or family, they need to come and get their treasures. I've seen too many clients stuck at the last minute with items promised to others who bailed on the responsibility of picking up what they were offered. Set boundaries. "I'd love for you to have x. Are you interested? Great. When can you come get it? It must be out a week before the move, and I have a charity coming on y day. If your item is still here, it will be waiting for you at Goodwill." Tough love is a motivator, especially for the procrastinators in our lives.

Media Mogul

Most children today have a huge media collection. If it's digital, you are in the catbird seat. It's coming along without your having to lift a finger. Your children may have a collection of CDs and DVDs that they enjoy. We're teaching organizing concepts this week, so based on what you did in the family room, decide what age-appropriate solution will work best here. But do cull the collection first! See page 164 for some pointers on the best ways to store media.

Fashionista Fling

Children are our mirrors. If you have too many clothes in your closet, your child most likely will too. If you purge your closet on a regular basis, I'll bet your child will too. Parents often ask me to begin organizing the home in their child's room, and I refuse. It's best to teach by example. I have never had a child see his parents' organized closet and not be impressed. All of them ask if they can have my help organizing their closets!

The guidelines are the same as for your wardrobe (see pages 91–93): Is the garment frayed, stained, missing buttons, or otherwise unwearable outside the house? Toss it. Has it been cast aside because it's no longer interesting or in vogue? Donate it. Hanging clothes will go into wardrobe boxes, and shoes will be tossed on the bottom. Dresser drawers can be left full, provided they hold only clothing. Again, clear that with your professional mover or the friends who are moving you. You can put moving paper over the items to keep them from shifting wildly. This is a great time to toss out old jewelry and makeup if your daughter is at that age.

Kids' Rooms Moving-Day Box

Once again I doubt you need one unless you have very young children who must have a few stuffed animals for comfort. I'd tuck them in with their sheets and towels and be all set with one less box to load. Of course, the treasure of the moment needs to be safely in little hands on the big day for security.

Planning for the Kids' Next Bedrooms

You have an amazing opportunity to help ease the transition by involving your children in the creation of their next living space. Draw the floor plan and measure the furniture that's going to be making the journey. Where will everything go? Do you need any new pieces? Can you shop for those items beforehand and have them shipped to the new address? Instead of just shifting everything over and recreating the present reality, perhaps create something fresh and new.

- Are all the school trophies still needed?
- Is it time for a new duvet cover or bedspread?
- Could items on the wall be retired and replaced?
- What about the furniture and window coverings? Will they work in the new room?
- What will the new theme be?

Engaging children in this way can make them feel like partners in the process rather than victims of a decision out of their control. Renters often fear painting the walls bold colors because they must restore them to neutral. But you can do one wall as an accent! What child wouldn't enjoy learning the power of color to create a new look, especially if the furniture, bedding, and window coverings are going to be exactly the same? As I have suggested multiple times, painting a table or chair changes the piece entirely. If your child is interested and old enough, he can do that before you move. If he is too young, you can make it a priority after you get settled. What a lovely project to share! Put it on the calendar to demonstrate that it's a reality. Children, just like adults, can find visual stimulation inspiring, so introduce them to Pinterest and Houzz. If you wind up with a professional decorator or architect, I'll be giggling with joy.

Zen Organizers Are Made Not Born

If your child has never been introduced to organizing tools, now is the perfect opportunity to open his world. Here are some great items any child can enjoy:

- Uniform hangers (use different colors for each child)
- Bins for specific types of toys
- Sweater drawers
- Over-the-door shoe organizers, shoe drawers, or shoe racks (depending on the age, number, and types of shoes)
- Space bags
- Drawer liners and small-drawer organizers
- A toy net over the bed and/or in the bathroom for stuffed animals (for very young children)

If you have older children you can teach them how to create a file system for their homework. Imagine how easy the transition will be to bill paying as an adult! Once again, the biggest boost to getting organized is an organized parent who models the desired behavior and makes use of the very same products. Children think that being an adult is all about buying whatever you want and staying out late at night. It's really about things like creating and maintaining an organized home to support whatever one wants to accomplish in life, being fiscally responsible, and preserving one's health. Those aren't very sexy to the average teenager, so, again, your example is key.

Memorabilia and the Art of Letting Go

Often we cannot sell or trade the treasures we amass over our lifetimes. To preserve the precious nature of these items, we should select them with great care. You don't need every piece of paper a now-deceased loved one ever touched to remember him or her; you need the loving note sent when you least expected that person to be thinking about you or that birthday card with the special message. If you are saving your child's artwork, schoolbooks, merit badges, and trophies, ask yourself if he or she will ever appreciate, want, or be able to house this collection when he goes off and creates a family of his own. In reality you are saving these items to hold on to a precious but fleeting part of your own history. The trick is to keep moving forward so that every phase of life is precious for different reasons.

Of all the items that parents grieve over parting with, baby clothes top the charts. Pregnancy and birth are life-changing experiences, and when a longed-for child arrives, it's truly a celebration. Time passes, and one day it becomes evident that the last baby has joined the family, whether that's a reality determined by age, finances, medical circumstances, or any other consideration. Then all those expensive baby items get wept over not because of their price or beauty but because they represent the end of a life phase. I would do my best to find someone special to give these items to so that you have a sense of sharing the joy with a new mother. Whether it's to a family member, friend, or charity, make those gifts before you exit this location. Do the same with baby cribs and the other nursery accoutrements. If you have a photo of your child in one of those special outfits, once again make a shadow box with a swatch of fabric from the garment she's wearing in the photo. If your daughter has baby dolls, perhaps one or two of the outfits will fit one of them.

A word of caution: it's best to make sure that items saved out of sentiment (especially for others!) will be used immediately. If not, consider whether the space might be more valuable than the emotional attachment. I have a client who promised her sister she would save her baby's things so that when her sister became a mom she'd be set. By the time the younger sister had a baby, however, the older sister's son was in high school. Those clothes were boxed up and stored for more than a decade. In fact, the boxes had their own garage. Yes, the car was parked in the driveway to accommodate a promise made long ago. And who could have known that a little girl would show up instead of another boy? Don't beat yourself up if you did something like this and feel foolish. It isn't a crime to delay decisions or waste space. As Maya Angelou said, when you know better, you do better. Just answer this all-important question and take action: Can you park in your garage?

Consider another example. I organize some homes once a year just to give the family a tune up. A particular home was a joy to clean out because it was designed by a famous architect and had a warm, welcoming feel. One year the tune up went well until we got to the children's rooms. They were both teenagers, and I was amazed to see the change in their wardrobes. They were truly young adults on the crest of going off to college. Between the two bedrooms was a play area. When they were young, this had been a magical place sweetly divided between them. Now orphaned toys littered the floor, while the bookcases held books for much younger children. This room revealed to me the struggle the mom was undergoing. Once cleared out and organized, this area would be used differently. The children must have sensed their mother's attachment because they didn't complain about not being able to use the area. They simply abandoned it.

No matter how quickly and easily my clients surrender items in the home, when it comes to their offspring, the game changes. The key is a balanced approach, and I think embracing the last line from the quote at the top of this chapter helps as well: "Remain in the simplicity of the present moment." It's easy to say but not so easy to do when the sorrows of the past and fears about the future hold us in their clutches.

If you have read my previous books, you may remember the story of the yellow slickers. I had a client whose every nook, cranny, drawer, cupboard, and closet was packed. She was sixty-one at the time and still had the cashmere sweaters she wore in high school. When I suggested she donate them, she said she planned to have them mended (moths had eaten a few holes). Sixteen- and a sixty-one-year-old bodies are very different, and the clothing appropriate for one doesn't usually suit the other.

The story of the two yellow slickers, however, taught me everything I needed to know about her and other clients deeply attached to certain possessions. My client regretted giving away the yellow slickers her sons wore the year the family lived abroad. She remembered the boys standing in the rain waiting for the school bus. Her sons were now grown men with families of their own. She had a lifetime of memories and a house full of memorabilia. Why even think about those slickers? I realized that for her the physical object was imbued with the memory and the experience. She had in fact turned it into a magic talisman. By giving it away, she believed on some level that she had given away the experience.

I worked with another client who was a serious saver. Her home was littered with the accumulated mementos of a lifetime. They lived in boxes, in closets, and in plain sight. They filled the garage and had even overflowed into rented storage spaces. Every single item was a treasure. This woman was not a hoarder, by the way. Her home was not cluttered with books, papers, and shopping bags full of stuff. The mementos were all hidden away or artfully on display. She imagined that "one day" she would give it all a coherent presentation. This is almost always the plan when someone can't let go. I subsequently read that some traumatized or depressed people feel that they are literally not fully present for their life experiences. An object represents the experience and serves to remind them.

Needless to say, if you recognize yourself in any of these extreme examples, perhaps consider a few sessions with a therapist to help you detach not so much from the object but from the fear that binds you to it—the anxiety that you will forget this time in your life or a particular experience without the object. The truth is that the experience lives inside you. If you feel you cannot sort your memorabilia and you have space to store it in the new home, then pack it in an organized fashion and make an action plan for after the move. Here's the stark reality: when people die, family members keep what is valuable and let go of the rest. You might as well sort and toss your own memorabilia. Your heirs won't thank you if you don't.

Children's Treasures

The vast majority of my clients will ultimately reduce their children's memorabilia to a precious few items. It's great to get small project boxes for each child from a place like The Container Store and put in some treasures, dedicating one box to each year of their lives. Now that we're all running around with phone cameras, it's easy to capture the moment and store it online at a site like Snapfish.com. You create a digital album and decide who can have access. It's a snap for all of your relatives and closest friends to see little Johnny and Mary change and evolve almost daily without your having to make copies and do a special snail mail project. Your children can visit those images for a lifetime. If your chosen site goes out of business, you'll have time to shift your collection elsewhere. Of course, there's also Instagram and Facebook and whatever other social media sites you frequent, but those may be of the moment and fleeting. Even at trusted social media sites, I would stay on top of shifting privacy settings and make sure that your children are being viewed by those you handpick and not the world at large. There are some strange folks out there. By the way, if you have relatives who insist on hard copies of photos, send the digital images to a store near them like Costco, and they can get all the prints they wish.

If you are a typical parent, you have thousands of images. Get them off the hard drive of your main computer and your phone and put them on a drive devoted to photos. I would also put them on a thumb drive and pop that into a safety deposit box or fireproof safe. You can update or add drives periodically. In a fire, photo albums are among the first things people grab, and people feel devastated when they are lost. If you are of a certain age, you don't just have digital clutter, you also have a box or two of photos waiting for the day you pop them into albums. I would not stop this week to create albums, but I would make it a point at the next location to schedule some time (or hire a service) to digitize those images. This will preserve your family history for your children.

While we're on the subject of preserving family history why not interview all family members, starting with the oldest, and create a living history? We all think we're going to remember the stories we hear a thousand times, but after someone dies, most of us realize the details have been lost. If the family gathers for big holidays or for an annual reunion, make it a point to do some interviews. And if you are the family historian, be sure your story is captured as well. A budding Spielberg in the family can edit these interviews into the ultimate home movie.

I grew up in a brownstone in Brooklyn. One day there was a neighborhood emergency, and everyone for several blocks was given minutes to exit. An explosion was feared. My father was home alone and grabbed two things. I love to ask people if they can guess what he grabbed. What would your guess be? What would you grab if given mere minutes to leave your home? My dad made an instant decision and knew where his treasures were. Being organized served my father well. What did he take? He grabbed a large envelope full of insurance policies because, he said, with those he could replace whatever was lost. And he grabbed our collie because he said life was precious and irreplaceable. My father liked to give lectures about life, but with this one action, he taught me volumes about what is truly valuable.

Off to College: Preparing for the Dorm

This book deals principally with big moves in which adults move their households to a new location. One of the first moves many young people make on the road to independence is to a college dorm room. Here are some guidelines for the college bound to prepare for this move—a rite of passage in many ways.

I like to think of this move as a primer. Life in a dorm is stripped down to the minimum. What will you need? In answering this question, start with what the college or university provides. The typical room has a desk, chair, extra-long single bed, and closet. Once you've been accepted, the college or university will send you a list of suggested items for the room. You'll find additional lists put out by most big-box stores, which of course want you to make your purchases from them. I have a few suggestions to add to these lists. These are the Zen Organizer's "don't leave home without 'em" items.

- One of the unwelcome guests you may find in your dorm room is a bed bug. If he's there, he's brought his entire family, and they are eager to feed on you. They are incredibly difficult to get rid of, so work from a prevention standpoint. Better safe than sorry indeed. Your dorm mattress will no doubt have served several students before you, so purchase a bed-bug-prevention mattress cover. If the mattress is infected, this will seal them in and keep them away from your skin. And don't forget to get a bed bug cover for your pillow! Zipper closures are the best for these items.

- Your mattress is likely in need of help when it comes to your getting a good night's sleep, so another solid investment is an egg-crate or Tempur-Pedic-style foam pad. You'll place that over the covered mattress and then use a mattress pad and your sheets.

- Invest in risers so you can have under-the-bed storage. Keep your suitcases there, for example, full of off-season clothing, or store your extra linens in them if you lack space elsewhere. If you store clothing there, use space bags to maximize the space.

- A clutter-free room that is dusted and vacuumed regularly will keep critters at bay. Being a slob, especially one who leaves food out, invites all sorts of creepy crawlies to invade your space. An organized environment has many payoffs, doesn't it?

- You should work with the big-box entity you trust. For me Bed Bath & Beyond (BB&B) offers the perfect solution. You go to a store location near you, shop with the help of an associate experienced in dorm living, and create a registry of items you need. Ask family and friends to give you gift cards for the store as a graduation gift. They can also purchase items directly for you. When you get to the campus, your items will have been pulled and will be waiting for you at the BB&B closest to campus.

- BB&B honors its discount coupons even after the expiration date, so use as many as you can. I have a friend who reduced her daughter's bill by $300. Are you reading between the lines here? The "B word" is once again rearing its head. Separate from tuition and books is the expense of putting together your child's first home away from home. Perhaps you will ask your undergraduate to cover the expense or to contribute with a part-time job; maybe you'll allow him or her just to enjoy the benefits; either way, it's good for kids leaving home for the first time to have an understanding of the finances involved.

- Two sets of sheets and towels, one in use and one waiting to be washed, are adequate. And you'll certainly want a good-size laundry bag.

- Use huggable hangers as they are narrow and take up less space. They are also kind to clothing and prevent items made of silk or with spaghetti straps from tumbling to the floor. Use one color for uniformity. If your roommate uses another, there will never be a question about ownership, will there?

- You'll want a comforter and possibly a blanket if your school is in a cold climate. BB&B has bed-in-a-bag sets, which are your most economical option.

- The dorm room will probably have a light for each of the desks. It's great to invest in one with built-in plugs and chargers. Once you're settled, see how many power strips you need.

- Have shower shoes and a caddy to take your toiletries with you. A Grid Tote is really perfect for this kind of transport, and your shower items will be safe in your room. You might also try a tote made of a thick rubber material; Rubbermaid is a great site to explore. If you're prone to dropping things, this is a safer, sturdier bet.

- The room may come with a small refrigerator. If you have the space, invest in your own. Even minimal food for two in such a small space can be a drag.

- Honor your personal quirks! For example, if you prefer to work in bed rather than at a desk, purchase a small portable workstation. This isn't great Feng Shui, so try to embrace working at a desk; otherwise, work and rest energies mix, and you may find yourself getting sleepy when it's time to study or wide awake when it's time to sleep.

- I hope you never need them, but a small fire extinguisher and a first aid kit are always welcome, no matter where you live. The Red Cross sells first aid kits, or you can create one tailored to your needs.

- Dorms aren't usually responsible for theft or damage, so leave your most expensive entertainment equipment at home. Contact your new roommate(s) and divide the purchases between you. You don't need multiple TVs in a room designed for study and sleep. Check your family's homeowner's insurance policy and see if the dorm room can be covered. And leave the family heirlooms at home.

- Resist the temptation to bring decorative items and sentimental pieces from home. You are in the enviable position of starting your life and discovering who you really are at your core, separate from your parents, their values, and their interests. Add mementos from your new life to this room. And if you really need to see mom, dad, siblings, and Fido, have their images rotate as your screen saver.

- When the academic year ends, the school may provide storage you can rent for the personal items you brought with you and will need again. Most large universities also have outside businesses nearby that can rent space to you. When you graduate, you can take these items with you to your first apartment (if it's nearby), sell them, or donate them.

I've saved the best for last. Setting up a dorm room is fairly mechanical. Getting stuck with someone you dislike is the nightmare everyone dreads. You will be asked to fill out a form that helps the university match you with another student. Very often students or parents complete those forms with information that they think makes them sound desirable but that has nothing to do with reality. If you go to bed at eight because you need a lot of sleep, say so. If you like to pull all-nighters as a matter of course, say that. You get the idea. It's not a guarantee, but it will move you closer to finding a compatible roommate than a fabricated form ever will.

I'd encourage you not to room with your "besties" from high school. Cliques will naturally form; you don't need to arrive with an intact unit. Open your world and make new friends. Encourage those you treasured at home to do the same, and soon you'll have an amazing network of new "besties." It's often the case that while one person is out making new friends, the other finds him- or herself crippled with shyness. You don't want to have to deal with jealousy, which sadly can be a by-product of keeping your tribe together. Expand rather than insulate, and invite everyone to join the fun.

I love that you can make this move without any shipping expenses, provided you have access to a Bed Bath & Beyond store. Other big-box stores can help. Needless to say, your friends at The Container Store may not have bedding and towels, but they do have organizing tools.

Dorm living can serve as a training ground for setting up a first apartment and arranging your own home in a way that pleases you; it also teaches you about sharing space with others. If you ultimately choose a partner, there will be a learning curve called compromise. You will know what you look like in a space courtesy of your possessions, and your partner will also have been expressing him- or herself in a unique way. What will the new "we" look like? It's an exciting adventure.

Parents, guide your undergraduate with respect to his or her interest in what the dorm room is going to look like and how it will function. The average teenager will take a wee bit more than needed to college, and life with experienced peers will be the best motivation to eliminate the excess. We can guide our children, but in the end some lessons are learned the hard way.

If college-bound students can embrace small-space living as a way of life rather than a temporary interruption in the habit of mass consumption, we may produce a generation with a new relationship to stuff. The recent Great Recession is supposed to yield a generation as fiscally conservative as that which came of age during the Great Depression. These two trends might work well together, which brings me to a look at how adults might embrace a slightly different version of small-space living—you know, one where you don't have to share a bathroom with a gaggle of teenagers.

The Circle of Life: Retirement

After the children leave home, you just don't need the same amount of stuff or as much room. In some ways, downsizing entails returning to the simple time that began our lives. Shakespeare expressed the journey in his sonnet about the seven ages of man. Instead of feeling like a big burden has been lifted, many people feel a tremendous sense of loss. I've discussed this in various ways throughout this book, but I'll say it again: you are not your stuff, and you are not defined by a particular time in your life. Our lives are ever evolving, and while I agree that we each need to honor our past, we should not let it eclipse the potential of the present to bring joy, fulfillment, and (heaven help us) different kinds of stuff.

If you are getting ready to retire, the downsizing instructions in this book are perfect for you. Your sweep through your current home will probably be a bit more stringent. Your move will most likely not be a lateral one by any description. Retirement comes for many these days in a series of steps. The big house, where the children were raised, gives way to a condo or ranch-style home. Retirement communities are popular now and begin taking folks in their early fifties. If you are a very outgoing person and want to have access to daily activities and an on-site staff of helpers, this may be the perfect choice. In addition, if something happens to your partner, you'll have a built-in community of neighbors.

It's wise to have a conversation with a financial planner (one who takes a fee rather than one who receives a commission on transactions made) and be sure you are heading for an enjoyable retirement. Everyone who owns anything of value, whether age twenty-five or seventy-five, needs a will. I realize in some cultures this is a verboten subject, but if you don't designate who gets your stuff, I assure you our beloved Uncle Sam will step in, and from the other side you are not likely to be pleased by the outcome. Once again, it's time to pull up those big-boy or big-girl pants and make a few calls. Your financial planner, tax attorney, insurance agent, and progeny all want to be in on the plan. I have a client whose parents made an airtight estate plan several years ago. The children are all outside the home, married with children of their own. The plan was revealed in detail to everyone so that any disagreement about disbursements could be worked out with the parents before their deaths. My friend is the appointed executrix. Every time she sees her parents, they quiz her to be sure she remembers how to proceed. I find this level of planning to be fiscally responsible, the ultimate act of love and a powerful example.

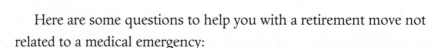

Perhaps the most painful move is to an assisted-living facility because it clearly marks the end of life's open choices. The residents generally have one large room to live in, and the end of this lifetime is on the horizon. Many facilities offer wonderful amenities, and there is no reason the rooms can't be appointed with prized possessions. Be aware that professional organizers have specialties. If you contact the National Association of Professional Organizers, you will be directed to your local chapter. I'm sure you'll find someone who specializes in retirement moves. In addition, you can engage services to help you sort your things, dispose of what you no longer need, and unpack you in the new space. I know of one called Smooth Transitions. We live in an era of abundant choices. If you have the funds, perhaps a combination team will serve you best.

Here are some questions to help you with a retirement move not related to a medical emergency:

- If your children are grown with families of their own, what kind of guest amenities do you wish to offer? Do you want them to stay in a hotel or with you?
- How many rooms do you now have? Will you need all of the furniture in them? Might friends or family members want to take some pieces off your hands? Most charities will take furniture in good condition, so you needn't be stuck. When you reduce the number of rooms, you need to remember to downsize things like window shades and blinds, curtains and drapes, rugs, wall art, and lights.

- Are you retiring to a warmer climate? You won't need all of your heavy sweaters, snow boots, and coats.

- Will you need to acquire a car, or are you moving to a city with a good public transportation system?

- Do you plan to entertain from time to time? Even if you do, you probably won't need the service for twelve or the cut-crystal glasses. Give them to the family member who will carry on the holiday traditions. Don't forget to give him or her the turkey roaster and thermometer. Let someone else baste for a change.

> If circumstances prevent you from taking your pets with you, please find new homes for them. City shelters are full of abandoned dogs and cats, and most lose their lives because no one took the time to find them a new family. If you have a specific breed of dog or cat, you'll find a rescue dedicated to that breed in your area. Its volunteers will take and rehome your pet. There are also organizations devoted to rescuing old pets. I've listed them in the resources section. It takes a little time, elbow grease, and legwork, but your creatures have devoted themselves to you, and securing the last phase of their lives is a fitting way to express your gratitude.

For those moving a family member into assisted living, make that person a part of the transition decisions as much as possible. This is a great time to scan photos and have an electronic photo frame that allows them to flash randomly on the screen. Be sure the bed is covered with a favorite bedspread or duvet. Life is in the details, and so are our memories. Here's a perfect example of being surrounded and comforted by select treasures rather than being overrun by every single item that ever meant anything to you. This kind of move is incredibly difficult but a thoughtful inspection of each room will give you focus and a modicum of control. That's the great gift of organization: when life is shifting around us, we can control the environment in which we live and the items we choose to populate it. In that way our surroundings give us support, peace, and the courage to carry on. When your emotions threaten to carry you away, you can instead focus on a bit of organizing to give your mind a place to rest.

Big Day on the Horizon

If you don't have children at home, you can use this week to catch up on any work you weren't able to accomplish up to this point. If you are up to date, you can look ahead to next week and get a jump on storage spaces. This is really a vast category, and you may think you have everything under one roof and be surprised to learn you have a homework assignment! When was the last time you went into the basement, checked the attic, looked in your outside storage unit, or visited your old room at mom and dad's house? See? You really do have more weeding and sorting to do.

If your children have left home and you've left their rooms intact for when they visit, the task this week will involve not only this chapter's instructions but also a conversation with your kids. They can certainly keep everything they left, but now the burden switches to them. Where and how will they house these items? You are not a free storage facility. Cut the cord. It's time to enrich your relationship and enjoy them as the productive, kind, and self-reliant adults you raised them to be.

If your kids want items from their rooms, they need to come get them or pay to have them boxed and shipped. I'm sure you can find a professional organizer to take this task off your to-do list. Having to pay the organizer and the shipping expense will give your children more incentive to choose wisely. If items need to be donated to charity, such as the bedroom furniture, offer them the tax deduction. They may not be aware of how one can use a swatch of fabric to bring a photograph alive in an album or how easy it is to combine memorabilia and make a shadow box. You can share many of the techniques you've learned in this book should your kids be more attached to stuff than you are. Parents never stop teaching by example.

- Be sure to arrange to have your current and next home cleaned.
- Do you have the keys yet for your new home? When do you receive them?
- How is the mover to be paid? If by certified check, have you scheduled a day to go to the bank?
- Are Fido and Fifi being boarded? Have you made those arrangements?

Week's Summary

- ❏ Talk to your child about the concept of self-care, and share with her a self-care tip.
- ❏ Do a speed elimination in your child's room, or if she is older, let her do her own.
- ❏ Organize your child's media collection.
- ❏ Purge the closet.
- ❏ Make plans for the next bedroom.
- ❏ Consider the hold all memorabilia has on us, but especially that pertaining to our children.
- ❏ Prepare for a dorm move.
- ❏ Downsize for a move to a retirement home, and think of this new life phase as a time of freedom.
- ❏ Make the move to assisted living as smooth and comfortable as possible.

A Closing Thought

The move is on the horizon. Don't allow anyone to slow your progress. You are in the process of creating something new and fresh. Loved ones who have left stuff in your home are now free to embark on that same journey. They must integrate those items into their own homes. You don't have to move to create a seismic shift in your home environment. In real estate the mantra is "Location, location, location." For a professional organizer, I'd say it's "Decisions, decisions, decisions." For those affected by your move, perhaps it's "Growth and freedom." And that's a great note on which to bring our week to a close.

HIDDEN POCKETS OF UNMADE DECISIONS AND FINAL PLANS FOR THE BIG DAY

> We must be willing to get rid of the life
> we've planned, so as to have the life
> that is waiting for us.
>
> —JOSEPH CAMPBELLL

I THINK OF THIS QUOTE IN A SLIGHTLY ALTERED FASHION THAT I hope the late Mr. Campbell would approve: we must be willing to get rid of the stuff we've collected, so as to have room for the stuff that is en route to us. When people don't know what to do with an item, it goes to the garage, attic, basement, or off-site storage. We attack these this week as experienced Zen organizers. If we did this work in week one, you might be more inclined to further postpone the decisions about these orphaned items. Now the move is closing in, and your need to be free should be much stronger than your need to hang on.

SELF-CARE TIP OF THE WEEK

THERE WILL BE a lot more hauling and lifting this week, so my self-care tip is to get some kind of body treatment. I have gone for regular acupuncture, massage, and chiropractic for many years. I don't know how I would cope without their restorative power.

The Secret Dump Site: Packing the Garage

I'm always amazed when I drive through a beautiful neighborhood filled with expensive, well-maintained homes to see a garage door open to reveal a scene out of some horror movie. Your garage is part of your home's energy. It's certainly counted in the square footage. And yet it is treated, for the most part, like a dumpsite. Let's do a little tossing and sorting so that you aren't taking unnecessary items to the new garage. And let's make a plan for the new space so you don't recreate this horror.

What belongs in the garage?

- A car (although 90 percent of the garages I organize hold junk and the car(s) live outside in the elements)
- Gardening equipment and supplies
- Tools
- Sports equipment
- Seasonal holiday items
- An extra refrigerator or freezer
- Automobile supplies

- Household supplies like cleaning products, toilet paper, tissues, and paper towels
- Emergency supplies for earthquake, fires, floods, and so forth

You might have a category unique to you. For example, perhaps you converted part of the floor space to a studio where you paint, dance, or exercise. Or maybe you run a home-based business and store products in the garage. In other words, there are legitimate additions, but don't go crazy and make all the miscellaneous detritus in your garage a legitimate category. Take a minute to list your categories, limiting them to the items you need to store in the next garage.

Here are some questions about your next garage:

- What does the new garage have? Be specific. How many shelves? How many cabinets? What are their measurements?
- Has it been professionally designed with built-in cabinets and shelves? (This is the ideal but certainly expensive. If you bought the home, it's worth considering.)
- Does it have a loft for storage?
- Are there hooks on the walls to hang items like bicycles?
- Is there a pulley system to fly specialty items like a surfboard?
- Do you have free wall space to be creative with? You can measure your garage, make a list of items you need to store, and go to The Container Store or IKEA for a free space plan. They can of course sell you the systems and storage bins you'll need.

The least expensive way to make an empty garage more storage and user friendly is to go to a place like The Home Depot and buy heavy-duty shelving units, as well as products that allow you to hang items like bikes and tools with handles (e.g., brooms, mops, shovels).

The main rule of thumb is that the floor should be kept clear and categories of items kept together. When the holidays roll around, you don't want to be digging into stacks of boxes looking for your deco-rations. You want to go to one shelving unit and know that all of your Christmas/Chanukah/Kwanza boxes are together. If you must stack boxes, use storage tubs on wheels. When you need holiday boxes (or any other category that generally fills multiple containers), you can pull the entire group out with one effort as it's all in one stack. By the way, while keeping the floor clear is an aesthetic choice, it's also a practical one. In the event of a flood, you won't have to worry about ruined boxes.

Rats, roaches, raccoons, and all manner of creatures and creepy crawl-ies love to feast on paper. Cardboard is like a thick, juicy steak. Rather than storing items in cardboard boxes, invest in heavy-duty plastic or rubber containers. Yes, rats can eat through just about anything, but at least you're buying time. And if the garage next door is a paper haven, they won't need to stop at your place. I'm not a fan of rat poison by the way because it finds its way into nature and can disrupt the ecosys-tem. Snakes are a rat's natural predator, and when they consume one with poison in its system, they die, in turn infecting the birds who eat them. Set some humane traps if rats are an issue, or call a service. In Los Angeles the rats can be trapped and taken to landfills.

Think ahead and plan the distribution of items so that seasonal things go in the back and what is accessed frequently stays in the front. I like to see shelves by the garage entry door to the home for storing extra paper products. These get used quickly, so I'm not too worried about them. But if your consumption of paper products is slow, for example, I'd pop them into large rubber tubs for long-term preservation. I learned the hard way that covered storage doesn't provide the surefire protection you may imagine. When my parents retired, they left Brooklyn for the Allegheny Mountains outside Pittsburgh. The house sat on three acres and had lots of storage sheds. In one shed far from the main house and rarely accessed except during the holiday season, I once unpacked our family's Christmas manger to find a nest of field mice and several babies. We never used that manger again. Invest in proper storage containers. If you are concerned about treasured items, find safe storage inside your home. Inspect holiday storage each year.

Hang as many items as you can. Most people fly their bikes on hooks. I, on the other hand, love to see bikes in kickstands. I think it makes them more accessible. This is an example of the kinds of choices you get to make so that your garage is enjoyably organized.

Finally, let me say a word about emergency supplies. In Los Angeles just about everybody has a stash in case of an earthquake. Emergencies (e.g., floods, tornadoes, hurricanes) hit every part of the country, so it's wise to have water, some canned or dehydrated food and perhaps a few packages of emergency rations, emergency blankets, and the like, on hand. I find my clients tend to store these items and then never check the expiration dates. Once a year, when you move your clocks forward, check all battery-operated items in the home, like smoke detectors. Check the expiration dates on canned goods and other food staples. And check on those emergency items. When the water expires for humans, your plants will enjoy it. Store your emergency kit where it will be easily accessible. If you Google "emergency preparedness," you will find the myriad ways people prepare for disaster. Whether you settle for water and some emergency rations or add camping equipment and big-ticket items like a generator is up to you. You don't have to handle this particular detail until after your move, but put a reminder on your calendar. It's too important to let slip through the cracks.

The garage is never the first room unpacked, so you have a bit of time after you get to the new space. Once you have your plan in place, whether it's high-end or down and dirty, you will be ready to get on your feet and start digging through the rubble of the current garage. If the weather is mild, open the garage door and place items in separate areas outside to see just how big each category is. If you know that most of the contents are going to be tossed, don't try to use your everyday trash cans. Rent a dumpster, fill it up, and have it hauled away.

If you are downsizing for a future move, you might have the time to check each box and transfer items like holiday ornaments to sturdier permanent containers. I'm personally not a fan of red or green containers for holiday storage. Later you won't be able to use them for other types of storage without being annoyed that you are constantly reminded of Christmas. You can photograph all manner of items, including Christmas ornaments, if it's time to say farewell. If you don't make these decisions, one day all of this stuff is going to be tossed into a dumpster by relatives or friends. Protect the future: eliminate as much of the past as you can now.

The Kingdom of Unmade Decisions: Packing the Attic and the Basement

With few exceptions, attics and basements become nothing more than additional storehouses for unmade decisions. They are like indoor garages in that they become dumping grounds. You probably have a lot of the past stored in these places, and having read this far, you now have more tools to help you make decisions about items with emotional value. Understand that you don't need every item in a sentimental category. Two or three can pay homage to the person or event now in the past, and you can find myriad ways to display or store items for future generations. You can investigate acid-free papers and other materials designed for long-term storage on the websites of The Container Store or Amazon. Paper disintegrates over time, so digital copies and digital scrapbooks really are the way to go. You store your photos on the Cloud or on a website rather than in your home (although a hard drive dedicated to images would make me sleep easier at night). And family and friends can enjoy the images once they're out of the attic.

I've seen attics that were crawl spaces and others that were full rooms (usually filled with furniture). The size of your attic will determine how much time this is going to take. Hopefully you'll whip through things quickly. This area tends not to be insulated, so if stored items have been damaged or have become mildewed and moldy, bid them farewell. The basement is also often dark and damp. Your best bet with both areas is to pull things out and keep them in categories. Don't forget to make liberal use of the dumpster or your friendly neighbor's additional trash cans. (I assume you're asking first.) You may not realize how much you have of something until you see it with its brethren.

Here are some questions to help you make quick work of the stuff you stored in these locations:

- Do you want these items in the next house?
- Do you have the correct containers?
- Should these things simply be tossed, given away, or donated? Are you going to use that treadmill in the new space? Is skiing in your future now that you're moving to Florida? You get the idea.
- Might any one category increase at the new location. If this is a retirement move, for example, you may finally be able to put

a workbench and a tricked-out tool area in the garage. Down-sizing doesn't indicate a loss; it announces a shift. Instead of eighty-hour workweeks, you now have twenty or thirty hobby hours to fill in a week.

This is the final week, so there's no time to belabor decisions. If you were sick of your own possessions about two weeks ago, pretty much nothing is sacred at this point. And remember that just because a house has a basement and an attic, these don't have to be chock-full of stuff. As a matter of fact, you don't have to store anything there. I know—for some people, having clear space in the home is a radical idea. Hold your tongue if the temptation arises to store furniture or other goods for a child, relative, or friend. There's always one good soul in a group who does and then usually gets stuck with that extra stuff for decades.

Finished basements, while rarely seen on the West Coast, are commonplace in the eastern United States. In many ways they were the precursor of today's family room. Every home used to have a formal living room, and if you wanted to let it all hang out, you went to the basement. Now, as a nation, we've pretty much eliminated the formal living room, and we all have a family room. Why not make a finished basement, if you have one, into a combo room? You could have your treadmill and free weights down there, along with a day bed for guests or maybe a space devoted to crafts. The world—or at least the basement—is your oyster.

If you use your basement as the family room, you probably organized it a few weeks ago. If you plan to use a finished basement in the next house as a crash pad for your teens, ask them for help in designing the new room. People have a greater sense of ownership and pride in keeping a room organized if they had a hand in deciding what it contains and how it's all to be used. Whatever is in this room, we've surely covered it in a previous week. Review those instructions, be ruthless, and have at it!

It's also good to review the placement of your furniture in the new home. As moving day approaches, do you now think that some furniture might be better served in a different part of your new abode? Decide now rather than on moving day. Your movers will no doubt be happy to rectify one or two mistakes in your decorating scheme, but they will get a bit snarky if they sense you have no real idea where things go. Sometimes a big tip isn't enough.

'Twas the Night Before . . . the Big Move!

Don't panic if you suddenly remember that you forgot to do something. It's bound to happen because you're human. Forget the recriminations and just find and implement a solution. The worst-case scenario will find you not able to distribute some last-minute items in a conscious way. Depending on where you live, you might even be able to put those items out on the street for random pickup. I once got a young couple to divest themselves of about 25 percent of the furniture in their apartment. There was too much in the space, and some of those pieces were from previous relationships. We had a camera crew coming the next day, so we were a bit unsure where it was all going to go until we remembered that we were in New York City. We put the items on the sidewalk, and within an hour everything had been taken. Instant recycling. What can I say? That's my hometown.

As long as the movers (whether professional or your friends) are on schedule and your utilities will be turned on, you have the basics covered. Your last-on, first-off boxes should be ready, and you should have proper payment for the movers and cash for tips. Does someone in the family need to make a run for water or food?

I don't mean to sound Pollyannaish, but in the midst of my worst experiences in life, I have found a gift. Look for it when things go awry.

Tips to Avoid Injury and Promote Happiness

- I've stressed self-care during the eight weeks of preparation. For moving day, it's critical. Get a good night's sleep. Eat a great breakfast. Order lunch for everyone and provide healthy snacks. Have an ocean of bottled water so everyone stays hydrated.

- Professional movers know how to lift, but you may have to remind your friends to lift with their legs not their backs. There's no time for a visit to the emergency room!

- Check the weather service, and be prepared for whatever Mother Nature sends your way. In fact, keep an eye on the forecast for a week in advance. You can't afford to be caught off guard. Most moves happen in the summer, so get an early start to avoid the most intense heat of the day.

- Don't stay up all night unpacking at the new location. You'll be exhausted, not making the best decisions, and moving more slowly than you realize.

- Everyone involved will have your new address, but not every GPS system is perfect at finding places. Use an online site like Mapquest.com, and print out directions or e-mail them the night before so that no one wastes time getting lost.

The Big Day

- Have coffee and donuts ready for your crew. I'm a health freak myself, but there's no sense serving yogurt and granola if the crowd wants carbs and sugar for energy. Again, be sure to eat a good breakfast. You need to be fueled for a long day.

- Have a plentiful supply of water. Half can be room temperature and the rest cold. You can adjust that if it's 110 degrees in the shade or if your movers like to chew ice chips. (Yes, I am kidding.)

- Be ready for the movers. They are going to ask you a thousand questions today, and you want to be available rather than working on a project that should have been completed weeks or days ago. If you did forget something, it won't be the first time they've encountered the issue. They will help you solve the problem.

- At both ends, a bathroom should be stocked (soap, toilet paper, paper towels, and a trash bag) and designated for the crew. If you are leaving or going to a big house, put a sign on the door so they will remember which one is for them.

- Stress the importance of the last-on, first-off boxes and any wardrobe boxes.

- Be sure to explain any packing codes so they mean something to the crew.

- As you walk out the door for the last time, be sure to turn off the lights and the stove. Close and lock all exterior doors and windows. Ensure that your utilities are scheduled for shut off that night and that service in your new location is scheduled to start that day. Oh, do you have your new keys, or is the new management waiting to greet you?

- Do a final sweep of each room with your driver. Movers take everything. I've seen them pack trash and full ashtrays. You don't want them taking something that belongs to the apartment. Don't forget to check your storage area outside the apartment or your parking spot.

- If you are leaving a rental, be sure you return to management all the keys you were given when you moved in, including any mailbox keys and garage remotes.

- At the new home, once the boxes are off the truck and the furniture has been placed, your movers will set up the beds. (Aren't you glad you have a bedroom box with your linens ready to make the bed?)

- Eat healthy snacks at regular intervals and continue to drink water—there's a reason I've mentioned water many times, as it truly is important to keep up your energy and stay hydrated today.

- If you rented a truck and moving aids like blankets and a dolly, be sure you know when they have to be returned. Don't incur unnecessary charges.

Your boxes are all labeled; however, make life easier for the movers and reduce the number of questions you'll be asked by putting up a sign on the door to each room announcing what goes inside. I call these "mover alerts." Upon arrival you will most likely take the lead guy or gal on a tour. He or she can do a lot of the directing, but mover alerts are great. If you are moving to a one-bedroom apartment, you won't need them. If you are moving into a big house, they will save you time, money, and energy.

Should you encounter broken items in the presence of the mover, be sure you photograph them immediately. We all have cell phones with cameras these days. If you encounter breakage within a box, document that as well. Find out how much time you have to notify the mover. If you stack those boxes up in the garage and unpack them two years later, your coverage will have lapsed. That's a great reason to get unpacked and organized! When I moved three hundred miles, I used a nationally recognized mover. Unfortunately my dining room table was broken in transit. In short order they had an extraordinary team out to repair it. They even left me with the best furniture polish I've ever used. Don't worry about damages because they are bound to happen. A reputable company will take good care of you.

THE BILL OF LADING

A professional mover will ask you to sign this document on the big day. Be sure to review it first and ensure that all the information shown is exactly what you previously agreed to when you chose this company. Here are some key items to be mindful of:

- Your mover's name and address or the name and address of the motor carrier issuing the bill of lading must be on the document. If your move involves changes of vehicles (as discussed in chapter 1), all vehicles need to be identified on this document.

- Contact information while the truck is in transit should be listed. (You and the driver should exchange cell phone numbers in the event of an accident, traffic jam, or other delay.)

- The form of acceptable payment needs to be indicated. You negotiated this when you got your estimate. Be sure it's the same; otherwise, the driver may refuse to unload the rig.

- Your bill of lading may have additional attachments, including the order for service, a binding or nonbinding estimate, and the all-important inventory of your goods. Keep these documents together.

- Be sure the destination address is correct.

You should designate one person as the keeper of the bill of lading and related documents. You need your inventory as you unpack. If your move is for work and is a tax-deductible expense, you want to keep this with your cancelled check or other receipt. Uncle Sam might one day ask for proof, and you want to be prepared, right? And don't forget to corral all the other move-related expenses if this is indeed a tax-deductible expense. If it isn't, tally the receipts at the end to be sure you did not go over budget.

Unpacking and the Period of Adjustment

No matter how delighted you are to have made this move, you can expect a rocky period. Take it in stride. It's part of the mourning process; after all, when you leave a residence, you also leave behind experiences, memories, and perhaps even loved ones. Self-care will continue to be critical, as will realistic expectations about the time it will take to get out of boxes and have all the details settled. My last move was very difficult because it involved a tremendous amount of downsizing. At one point I felt that every day of my life would forever be about some aspect of moving. When you have a plan, however, you can look at the calendar and see that a time is coming when you will just wake up and live your life without having to unpack a box, contact a corporation, or measure for an appliance or window treatment. The trick is to take the time to craft that plan. When you don't, you become the person who has thirty unpacked boxes in the garage from the last move.

The key rooms to unpack ASAP are the kitchen, bedrooms, and bathrooms. I start unpacking the minute the moving truck leaves the driveway and work to finish in record time—but this may not be right for your family if you need to take a breather. The family room, guest room, guest bathroom, and any bonus areas, like a finished basement or garage, can wait for a week or two. Settle in. Listen to the house's sounds; every home has its creaks and moans. Fill the new space with music, laughter, and conversation. Schedule time to work on every room. Delegate as many tasks as you can, whether to a human being in your home, someone you hire, or an online shopping site. There is no question that a professional organizer who specializes in moving can get you out of boxes in no time. My personal best is just over two hundred boxes in two and a half days, working with a crackerjack assistant and sleeping on-site. Many families move on a Friday and leave after the furniture is placed. They return Sunday night to a settled home with nary a box in sight. It's costly, but you should know the service is available. I'm not the only pro who loves to unpack other people's boxes and help create a home.

Here are some tips for unpacking in the days after your move:

- I like to unpack the kitchen first, and I'm happiest when I have the coffeemaker and toaster (or, even better, the toaster oven) in place. Most of us have a morning ritual, and it's comforting to know that on the first morning in your new home you'll be able to honor the way you like to start your day. Tailor your activities to make that possible. You won't need the deep fryer or the rolling pin for a bit.

- Have someone put your clothes away so the dress packs or wardrobe boxes can leave with the movers. If you organized your closet before you moved, this will be much easier because clothing will be packed in categories. If you are a super organized person, you can make a diagram showing your friend where items go in the new closet.

- One of the fastest ways to make progress is to work one room at a time. You don't have to complete it, but you can do the basics. Shove against the wall boxes that hold items you consider fine-tuning. For example, I wouldn't worry about books or media on day one. I'd want my pots and pans put away, but my memorabilia and craft supplies could wait until day two or three. This is a marathon not a sprint. If you see steady progress, you will be motivated to keep going.

- Look around and you'll see some very large boxes. If they were packed by the movers and are rather light, I'm going to bet they contain lampshades. They will be marked. Unpack these boxes to gain space; those boxes can exit with the empty wardrobe boxes.

- One of the most powerful ways to feel you are making progress is to have someone on hand whose sole job is to cut down the boxes and check the packing paper you are ready to discard. You don't want to throw out the cover to a sugar bowl because you're working quickly. This is a great job for a responsible friend or even a teenager. As boxes exit your home, you will feel the progress you are making. A sea of boxes is an overwhelming visual.

- Be sure you have a plan in place for the empty boxes. Are you giving them away? Do you plan to sell them? Will the mover come back to get them, or should your friend be breaking them down and keeping sizes together? Have this decided, and you will be grateful.
- Everyone needs box cutters. Period!

If you frequent chain stores, start shopping at the branch nearest you. It will be comforting to see the name of your favorite grocery store and know the products carried, even if the layout is different and you don't yet know the staff. Say hello to your neighbors and ask for recommendations for a dry cleaner, babysitters, or a doggie day care. After a few months the feeling that you have always lived here will replace any initial melancholy, and you will feel at home.

When your move is over, you'll want to dispose of your packing materials responsibly. Why not post an ad on Craigslist.org or Freecycle.org and offer the boxes and paper to someone? I'd narrow the window during which they can be picked up because you don't want to deal with flaky people who will leave you in the lurch. I'd also have everything cut down and the paper stuffed into a big box or a series of trash bags. I would not invite strangers into my new home to break down boxes. Needless to say, never engage in conversations about how many people occupy the new home, what you do for a living, or how friendly your dog is. Leave Fido in another room barking his head off. No stranger has to know he's a cream puff.

Most municipalities will give you one extra trash pickup for free after a move, so you have another option on the table. Place a call to the local trash service or visit its website to find out what's possible. Breaking down boxes and tying them together (usually by size) is backbreaking work. If you know any strong teenage boys who want to make a few extra dollars, this is the perfect task for them. The paper could be flattened, but I'd just stuff it into garbage bags and put it in the recycle bin if no one wants it. You need to safeguard your possessions, and not everything can be rolled in your towels and sheets. I encourage you to find a way to get these materials to another person facing a move. It's the ultimate recycle. I'm also realistic, however, and know that scenario isn't always easy to realize.

Week's Summary

- ❑ Clear clutter and pack the garage, attic, and basement.
- ❑ Plan for storage areas in the next home.
- ❑ Prepare for moving day:
- ❑ Set aside first-on, last-off moving-day boxes.
- ❑ Make sure your labeling system is in place.
- ❑ Have moving-day supplies (bottles of water, snacks) ready.
- ❑ Pack any remaining items.
- ❑ Move!
- ❑ Begin unpacking and getting rid of boxes.

A Closing Thought

At the end of a big undertaking like a change of residence, you need to have a reward to look forward to when the going gets tough. And trust me, no move is perfect, not even if you're a professional organizer. Have your reward in mind before you meet with a moving company, put the first box together, or fill out the change-of-address form at the post office. When times are tough, it's a great motivator to be able to think ahead and imagine yourself on your favorite beach, away for a theater weekend in New York City, or having a massage.

If it's possible, do a ceremony in each home to mark the official end of one journey and the start of another. You can look to your spiritual home or your ethnic heritage for traditional customs. The American Indians burned sage, and I think no matter what your background, you can enjoy this ritual. Home is a state of mind, not a physical structure. Whether you're moving to a 350-square-foot micro-apartment or a 9,000-square-foot mansion purchased with lottery winnings, that's your home. And it should feel like sacred space.

Light one end of a sage stick (readily available online or at Whole Foods), let it burn for a bit, then blow out the flame. As you move from room to room, you may want to have a small dish with you to catch the falling ash. Wave the stick to release smoke into the room. I like to move my hand in circles. In both spaces, ask that all negative experiences and memories be expunged. In your new home, ask that all who enter honor the space, respect your values, and nurture the hopes and dreams you have for the life you will create within these walls. Before you exit a room, trace the outlines of the doors and windows with the smoke to seal them against negative energies. Feel free to do this ancient ritual with an open heart. Even if it's far outside your normal experience, it's an ancient tradition and can't hurt anyone or anything. At the very least, your home will smell like Thanksgiving.

I'd like to close with a bit of Native American wisdom. May these words bless and guide the next phase of your journey:

Give thanks for unknown blessings already on their way.

Regina Leeds
Los Angeles, California
2014

A NOTE FROM REGINA

OUR JOURNEY TOGETHER HAS JUST BEGUN.

As promised I have additional information waiting for you at ReginaLeeds.com. I'll be updating the website regularly, so you'll always have access to the latest tips and products to help streamline your move. When you stop by the site, be sure to peruse my blog for organizing tips you can use in your new home. You'll also find information about my other books.

If you're keeping a digital notebook for your move, you'll find some checklists I created just for your move. Feel free to copy and paste them to your notebook and tailor them to your personal needs. You can use these as a jumping-off place to spark your own creativity. In fact, I invite you to send me your tips and tricks, and I'll share them with the Zen Organizer community via Facebook and Twitter.

When it comes time to shop for products, remember to check out my Zen-Organized Life board on Pinterest. You'll find hundreds of examples of my favorite products, as well as tips and images from all over the Internet that exemplify my philosophy. I've also created a page at Pinterest that showcases the specific products I mention in

223

this book, so you won't have to look hard to find the image you need. Copy it to your notebook, and you can flash the image when you go shopping for an item I suggest. I've got some fun off-topic boards too, so spend some time with me at Pinterest (http://www.pinterest .com/zenorg1).

> To us, our house was not unsentient matter—it had a heart, and a soul, and eyes to see us with; and approvals and solicitudes and deep sympathies; it was of us, and we were in its confidence, and lived in its grace and in the peace of its benediction.
>
> —MARK TWAIN

RESOURCES

ANIMAL ADOPTION RESOURCES

The Sanctuary for Senior Dogs is based in Ohio. They have extensive information at their website to help you re-home your senior. www .SancturaryforSeniorDogs.org

The Grey Muzzle Organization improves the lives of at-risk senior dogs by providing funding and resources to nonprofit animal shelters, rescue organizations, sanctuaries, and other nonprofit groups nationwide. They are based in North Carolina. www.GreyMuzzle.org

If your dog is a specific breed you can google that breed and your area. For example, "Golden Retriever Rescue in Los Angeles" yielded this resource: http://www.grcglarescue.org.

A general search for no-kill shelters yielded several sources including: https:// www.animalhouseshelter.com.

DONATING

Clothing and Household Items

Access Books: www.accessbooks.net (provides books to schools, classrooms, and community libraries in Southern California)

Big Brother Big Sister Foundation: www.bbbsfoundation.org (accepts donated clothing in good condition)

Career Gear: www.careergear.org (provides professional attire for job interviews to disadvantaged men)

Cinderella Project: www.cinderellaproject.net (gives donated formal dresses to teenage girls who can't afford to buy a prom dress)

Dress for Success: www.dressforsuccess.org (provides professional attire to disadvantaged women for job interviews)

Give the Gift of Sight: www.givethegiftofsight.com (provides free prescription eyewear to individuals in North America and developing countries around the world)

Goodwill Industries International: www.goodwill.org (sells clothing and household goods)

Half: www.half.com (helps you sell your stuff)

Hungry for Music: www.hungryformusic.org (distributes used musical instruments to underprivileged children)

One Warm Coat: www.onewarmcoat.org (collects and distributes coats for free to those in need)

Operation Paperback: www.operationpaperback.org (sends gently used books to American troops overseas and to veterans and military families at home)

PaperBackSwap: www.paperbackswap.com (provides an online service for swapping books with others)

Planet Aid: www.planetaid.org (recycles used clothing and shoes and promotes environmental protection and sustainable development)

Reader to Reader: www.readertoreader.org (accepts books for children and teens and distributes to school libraries nationwide)

Salvation Army: www.salvationarmy.com (sells donated clothing and household goods)

Suitcases for Kids: www.suitcasesforkids.org (provides luggage for foster children who move from home to home)

ThreadFlip: www.threadflip.com (connects buyers with sellers, offering women a simple way to convert their closets into boutiques)

ThredUp: www.thredup.com (provides an online thrift shop for buying and selling quality used clothes)

Vietnam Veterans of America: www.pickupplease.org (accepts clothing, shoes, and accessories in good condition for children and adults)

Yerdle: www.yerdle.com (connects donors with grateful receivers)

Computer Technology

Computers 4 Kids: www.c4k.org (provides caring mentorship, structured computer training, a vibrant learning environment, and access to a computer at home for low-income youth)

National Cristina Foundation: www.cristina.org (helps donors of used computers and other electronic hardware to select a local charity or school in their area to receive their equipment)

Techlicious: www.techlicious.com (discusses the latest trends, apps, and products in the tech world)

World Computer Exchange: www.worldcomputerexchange.org (provides tested used computers to schools and community organizations in developing countries)

FINANCIAL

Finding a Financial Professional

Certified Financial Planning Board of Standards: www.cfp.net (grants CFP certification, the recognized standard of excellence for competent and ethical personal financial planning)

CFA Institute: www.cfainstitute.org (promotes the highest standards of ethics, education, and professional excellence)

Financial Planning Association: www.fpanet.org (advocates for transparency, clear information, and high standards of conduct among financial planners)

National Association of Personal Financial Advisors: www.napfa.org (provides a database of financial planners with a proven a level of competency)

Managing Your Money Day to Day

Dinkytown: www.dinkytown.com (provides free financial calculators)

Expensr: www.expensr.com (provides a free online personal finance application)

Mint: www.mint.com (allows users to track bank, credit card, investment, and loan transactions and balances, make budgets, and set goals)

Moneychimp: www.moneychimp.com (provides articles and interactive features that explain finance and investments in Roth IRAs, stocks, and bonds; provides calculators and definitions of investing terms)

Quicken: www.quicken.com (provides budget and money management software)

Obtaining Credit Reports and Reporting Identity Theft

Equifax: www.equifax.com; 1-877-576-5734 (provides credit reports)

Experian: www.experian.com; 1-888-397-3742 (provides credit reports)

Free Annual Credit Report: www.annualcreditreport.com; 1-877-322-8228 (provides credit reports)

Identity theft: www.consumer.gov/idtheft (provides detailed information about reporting identity theft)

TransUnion: www.transunion.com; 1-800-680-7289 (provides information about obtaining or disputing your credit report)

INSPIRATION AND INSTRUCTION

About: www.about.com (provides content that helps people solve the large and small needs of everyday life)

eHow: www.ehow.com (offers instruction for all aspects of life, including how to pack a box)

Houzz: www.houzz.com (provides design ideas and how-to instruction from organizers, designers, contractors, architects, and so forth)

Instagram: www.instagram.com (lets you check out photos from your favorite designers, organizers, and architects to see what's trending).

MapQuest: www.mapquest.com (offers maps and point-to-point directions)

Pinterest: www.pinterest.com (lets you make online pin boards to collect ideas for all types of projects, including images from fellow pinners or anywhere on the Internet)

YouTube: www.youtube.com (provides how-to videos about all aspects of life, including the art of moving and organizing)

MIND, BODY, AND SPIRIT

Ariel Joseph Towne, the Feng Shui Guy: www.thefengshuiguy.com; consult@thefengshuiguy.com (helps people transform stagnant spaces in their homes and minds into positive, intentional spaces)

Network Chiropractors, founded by Donald Epstein: www.donaldepstein .com (provides a gentle, nonforce method)

Health Journeys, from the Belleruth Naparstek Guided Imagery Center: www.healthjourneys.com (offers guided imagery, hypnosis, and other mind-body products, research, and information)

Mysteries: www.mysteries.net (provides information about meditation and yoga)

Self-Realization Fellowship: www.selfrealizationfellowship.org (provides information about meditation and yoga)

Transcendental Meditation: www.tm.org (provides information about meditation and yoga)

MEMORABILIA, PHOTOGRAPHS, AND SCRAPBOOKING SUPPLIES

Carolyn Simon Designs: www.carolynsimondesigns.com (collects wedding lace to turn into jewelry)

Exposures: www.exposuresonline.com (offers albums and scrapbooks)

Michael's: www.michaels.com (provides arts-and-crafts supplies)

Scrapbooking 101: www.scrapbooking101.com (provides a guide to the basics of scrapbooking)

MOVERS AND MOVING

ApartmentGuide: www.apartmentguide.com (provides apartment rental listings nationwide)

Delancy Street Movers: www.delanceystreetfoundation.org/hireus.php (trains ex-convicts and recovering addicts as teachers, general contractors, truck drivers, and movers)

Moving: www.moving.com (provides easy-to-use resources and tools to help with local, long-distance, and international moves)

MovingScam: www.movingscam.com (provides assistance finding a reputable mover)

MyMove: www.mymove.com (provides moving tips, checklists, and deals)

PadMapper: www.padmapper.com (helps with home and apartment research)

ProtectYourMove: www.protectyourmove.gov (provides a user-friendly database of interstate moving companies searchable by state or name, as well as consumer complaint histories and on-road safety performance records)

Safety and Fitness Electronic Records (SAFER) System: www.safersys.org (offers company safety data and related services)

Trulia: www.trulia.com (helps with home and apartment research)

Zillow: www.zillow.com (helps with home and apartment research)

OFFICE AND FILING SUPPLIES

Day Runner: www.dayrunner.com (provides a calendar system)

Exposures: www.exposuresonline.com (offers binders, magazine holders, and so forth)

FitterFirst: www.fitter1.com (offers ergonomically correct products)

Google Docs: docs.google.com (lets you create and share your work online and access your documents from anywhere)

Levenger: www.levenger.com (offers binders, calendars, magazine holders, and more)

Office Depot: www.officedepot.com (provides office supplies and furniture)

Office Max: www.officemax.com (provides office supplies and furniture)

Relax the Back: www.relaxtheback.com (offers ergonomically correct office furniture)

Staples: www.staples.com (provides office supplies and furniture)

Online Assistants

Elance: www.elance.com

oDesk: www.odesk.com

VirtualAssistant: www.virtualassistant.org

VirtualAssistants: www.virtualassistants.com

ONLINE AUCTION AND SALES SITES

Cash for CDs: www.cashforcds.com (lets you sell your CDs, DVDs, vinyl LPs, and games)

Craig's List: www.craigslist.org (provides free classified ads with sections devoted to jobs, housing, items wanted and for sale, and so forth)

eBay: www.ebay.com (offers items for auction online)

Online Photo Management and Sharing

Flickr: www.flickr.com

Picasa (from Google): picasa.google.com

Picasa Web: www.picasaweb.com

Shutterfly: www.shutterfly.com

Snapfish: www.snapfish.com

ORGANIZATIONAL APPS

AboutOne: www.aboutone.com (provides a space for managing memories and household information)

CareZone: www.carezone.com (helps keep everyone coordinated)

Cozi: www.cozi.com (lets multiple family members manage appointments and schedules)

Evernote: www.evernote.com (provides a workspace for collecting lists, webpages, documents, and so forth)

Genius Scan: www.thegrizzlylabs.com (puts a scanner on your cell phone)

Google Calendar: www.google.com/calendar (allows users to create multiple online calendars)

Pet Master Pro: https://play.google.com/store/apps/details?id=com.pet works.android.petmaster.b (provides an organizer for pet health and details)

Red Cross's free Pet First Aid: www.redcross.org/mobile-apps/pet-first-aid -app (puts veterinary advice for everyday emergencies in the palm of your hand)

Two Happy Homes: www.twohappyhomes.com (provides an organization tool for parents living in separate households)

PROFESSIONAL ASSOCIATIONS

Clutterers Anonymous: www.clutterersanonymous.net (provides assistance with weeding out your clutter based on the twelve steps of Alcoholics Anonymous)

Codependents Anonymous: www.codependents.org (provides assistance with anxiety based on the twelve steps of Alcoholics Anonymous)

Messies Anonymous: www.messies.com (provides assistance with organizing your life based on the twelve steps of Alcoholics Anonymous)

National Association of Professional Organizers (NAPO): www.napo.net (provides a database of local professional organizers)

RECYCLING AND GREEN SAVING

1-800-GOT-JUNK?: www.1800gotjunk.com; 1-800-468-5865 (removes just about anything—furniture, appliances, electronics, yard waste, and renovation debris—and makes every effort to recycle or donate items)

Battery Solutions: www.batteryrecycling.com (recycles all battery types nationwide)

Environmental Defense Fund: www.fightglobalwarming.com/carboncalculator.cfm (provides an online quiz to calculate your personal energy impact)

Environmental Protection Agency: www.energystar.gov (provides information about energy-saving upgrades that might earn you a refund at tax time)

Rechargeable Battery Recycling Corporation (RBRC): www.call2recycle.org; 1-877-273-2925 (recycles used rechargeable batteries and old cell phones)

ReuseIt: www.reuseit.com (provides expertise in sourcing merchandise from communities to benefit local nonprofit organizations while responsibly recycling to help the environment)

Freeycle: www.freecycle.org (helps users give and receive items for free to keep these items out of landfills)

Worldwatch Institute: worldwatch.org (provides globally focused environmental research)

REDUCING AND STOPPING UNWANTED MAIL

Direct Marketing Association (DMA): www.the-dma.org (reduces the total volume of mail for individuals who register for its Mail Preference Service)

SMART SAVING AND SPENDING

Auto Club: www.autoclub.com (provides multiple benefits, such as trip planning and low-cost insurance, with a paid membership)

Consumerist: www.consumerist.com (provides consumer advocacy and responds to the latest consumer news and trends; published by Consumer Reports)

Suddenly Frugal: www.suddenlyfrugal.com (shares ideas for selling castoffs to make money, offers coupons, and more)

Union Plus: www.unionplus.org (offers discounts and advice to union members)

SHOPPING

Amazon: www.amazon.com

Bed Bath and Beyond: www.bedbathandbeyond.com

Costco: www.costco.com

Crate & Barrel: www.crateandbarrel.com

Home Depot: www.homedepot.com

Jouer Cosmetics: www.jouercosmetics.com

IKEA: www.ikea.com

Lowes: www.lowes.com

Pier One Imports: www.pier1.com

Pottery Barn: www.potterybarn.com

Pottery Barn Kids: www.potterybarnkids.com

Solay Wellness: www.natural-salt-lamps.com

Target: www.target.com

The Container Store: www.thecontainerstore.com

Wal-Mart: www.walmart.com

Williams-Sonoma: www.williams-sonoma.com

TAX FORMS AND TAX HELP

1040 or 1040EZ forms: http://www.aarp.org/money/taxes/aarp_taxaide

IRS guide to keeping records: www.irs.gov/efile: www.irs.gov/Businesses /Small-Businesses-&-Self-Employed/How-long-should-I-keep-records

THE AUTHOR

Facebook: www.facebook.com/TheZenOrganizer

Pinterest: www.pinterest.com/zenorg1

Twitter: www.twitter.com/TheZenOrganizer

Website: www.reginaleeds.com

Houzz: http://www.houzz.com/pro/regina-leeds/__public

ACKNOWLEDGMENTS

Editor Dan Ambrosio put me through my paces for a full year before we embraced the idea of writing a book about moving. Thank you, Dan, for your wisdom and guidance. You chose a topic dear to my heart.

Claire Ivett works as Dan's assistant, and her goal is to be an editor. Judging from her notes on my original manuscript, I'd say she is already a gifted one. I hope this book gives her much deserved recognition.

Project editor Carolyn Sobczak was always organized and compassionate during the difficult process of turning a mere manuscript into a book. She carefully chose the right person for all the myriad details that bring polish and completion to the finished product.

No person in the creative chain is scarier to a writer than the copy editor. Jennifer Kelland preserved my voice, tweaked my punctuation, and became a dear friend in the process. Jennifer deserves special credit for creating the "kick-ass" Resource section.

Thank you to Jon Valk and Jonathan Sainsbury for designing a cover I loved from the first moment I saw it.

Kudos to Linda Mark, who designed the interior of the book. It's amazing how powerful a great interior layout is to the message a book seeks to convey.

I can't imagine the patience it takes to create an index. Bravo to Robert Swanson for the detailed one he created for *Rightsize!*

My thanks to proofreader Kay Mariea for helping us catch the wayward errors that forever threaten to slip through the cracks.

I send bouquets of gratitude to Kate Burke, who handles PR on all six of the books I've written for Perseus. Kate is tireless, full of joy, and never says no!

Kevin Hanover, Sean Maher, and Jillian Farrel work quietly behind the scenes to market my books long after the initial PR blitz that accompanies publication has ended. They are great at surprises, and I thank them for all their efforts on my behalf.

Agent Marilyn Allen transformed my career and guided me to Perseus and the distinction of being a *New York Times* best-selling author. Marilyn, how can I ever thank you for believing in me and seeing the potential of Zen Organizing when no one else did?

Katie McHugh Malm, thank you for all you taught me. You are a part of every book I'll ever write.

Rightsize! was born with the constant encouragement of one seventeen-pound rescue dog named Charlie. I met him doing volunteer work. He beat the odds and survived distemper only to worm his way into my heart. I was looking for a Great Dane.

Be open to the surprises life brings you.

INDEX